Variations on a Floral Theme

Cynthia Venn

Published in 1996 by Cynthia Venn,
3 Anker Lane,
Stubbington,
Fareham, Hants.
PO14 3HE

Illustrated & Designed by Robert Venn

Photography by Alister Thorpe

Technical adviser: Jonathan Venn

Typesetting & Repro by Woodfield Publishing Services, Bognor Regis, UK

Printed in Great Britain

N.B. *The sizes of all templates in this book should be checked against the measurements of your cakes before starting work as cake dimensions vary according to the thickness of Marzipan and Icing. Assess any variations/discrepencies and adjust your tracing/s by stretching or compressing designs to fit your cake/s.*

Introduction

Floral themes are undoubtedly very popular throughout the world and this is probably due to the important role flowers play in most celebrations. The tradition of decorating churches with flowers for a wedding creates a beautiful background for the ceremony.

The language of flowers can convey many messages, from a declaration of love, the joy of a wedding, to a new arrival or a joyous homecoming.

The Ancient Chinese used flowers in all their religious rituals; each individual flower had a special meaning and originally each flower arrangement only included one flower.

The Greeks and Romans used flowers and leaves in all their celebrations, making headdresses, wreathes and garlands for brides and grooms and often sprinkled the ground in front of returning heroes with scented rose petals.

In the Far East, flower heads are strung together into necklaces and in the Pacific Islands the necklaces are given to visitors to welcome them.

Since Pagan times May Day has been celebrated with a Maypole garlanded with flowers and ribbons and young girls dance around it holding the end of the ribbon which is woven around the Pole in a pattern as they perform.

I am pleased to present this new collection of floral cake designs which I hope will stimulate busy cake decorators who have little time for experimenting into trying something a little different and maybe developing these designs into something of their own.

This book is dedicated with love
to Jessica Hannah, our
beautiful granddaughter.

Contents

Recipes

PASTILLAGE *(for Modelling & Plaques)*

1 lb (450g) Icing sugar
1 teasp. (5 ml.) Gum Tragacanth
3 tabsp. (45ml.) cold water
1½ level teasp. gelatine

🐦 Warm the sugar and Gum Tragacanth. Pour the water into a small basin and sprinkle on the gelatine. Allow to stand until all the water has been absorbed. Place the basin over a saucepan of hot water and leave until all the grains have been dissolved. A microwave oven may be used but be careful not to boil. Add to the sugar and mix with a 'K' beater. If a little dry add a drop more water.

SMOCKING PASTE

1lb (450g) Sugarpaste (rolled fondant)
½ teasp. (½ 5ml. spoonful) Gum Tragacanth
White vegetable fat

This paste would also be suitable for making a flounce or Garrett Frill when extra strength is required.

🐦 Grease hands liberally with white fat. Knead the Gum Tragacanth thoroughly into the sugarpaste. Place paste in a strong plastic bag and leave for a few hours before using.

FLOWER MODELLING PASTE

1lb (450g) Icing (confectioner's) sugar
5 teasp. (25ml) cold water
3 teasp. (15ml) Gum Tragacanth
2 teasp. (10ml) white vegetable fat
2 teasp. (10ml) powdered gelatine
2 teasp. (10ml) liquid glucose
1 egg white (large)

🐦 Sift the sugar and Gum Tragacanth into an ovenproof bowl. Heat gently in the oven or over a pan of boiling water until the sugar feels warm.

🐦 Sprinkle the gelatine on to the water and stand until the gelatine has absorbed all the water. Dissolve over hot water or in a microwave oven. Do not allow the mixture to boil as this would destroy the elasticity. Remove from the heat and add the fat and liquid glucose.

🐦 Pour the liquids and the egg white into a well in the centre of the sugar mixture. Mix in a heavy duty electric mixer on the slowest speed until the sugar has been incorporated. (The use of a dough hook will place less strain on the mixer). Increase the speed to maximum and mix until the paste is white and stringy. This will take 5-10 minutes. Put the paste into a strong polythene bag and keep in a lidded container overnight. As this paste dries out very quickly, it must be kept covered. To use, cut off only the small quantity required and knead it well before using. Store the remaining paste in the refrigerator. It can also be frozen.

GUM GLUE

2 teasp. (10ml) Gum Arabic
4 teasp. (20ml) rose water

🐦 Put the Gum Arabic and rose water into a small pot. Set the pot in a pan of hot water. Stir until dissolved. This is a good alternative adhesive when it is not desirable to use egg white.

EXTRA STRONG GUM GLUE

This is a very strong fast setting 'glue' suitable for sticking together dry petals. It is also very useful for invisibly repairing broken petals as it can be made exactly the same colour as the flower by using the same paste as a base.

🐦 Place a small piece of flowerpaste on a board. Add a drop of gum glue or egg white and mash these together to make a sticky substance which will dry quickly.

GLAZE (for leaves)

Isopropyl Alcohol with Confectioner's Varnish

Proportions:

*¾ **strength glaze*** = ¾ confectioner's varnish / ¼ Alcohol
*½ **strength glaze*** = ½ confectioner's varnish / ½ Alcohol
*¼ **strength glaze*** = ¼ confectioner's varnish / ¾ Alcohol

🐦 Add the Isopropyl Alcohol by dribbling a little at a time to the varnish, shaking it well. Repeat until all the alcohol has been added. (**Vodka** may be used as a substitute alcohol).

Techniques

TRANSFERRING A DESIGN BY EMBOSSING

This method is very useful for transferring designs and is very successful when used for the top of a cake.

It should be noted that the result will be a mirror image of the design so if it is important, as in the case of lettering or a design which is difficult to follow, that the image on the cake is exactly the same as the pattern. Trace over the back of the pattern and place that side face up under the perspex.

REQUIREMENTS

A piece of perspex larger than the surface of the cake. *(The perspex should be grease-free otherwise the icing will not stick to it.)*

Nº 0 or 1 tube.

White Royal icing.

- Place the design under the perspex.

- Pipe over all the outlines neatly, making sure that you do not leave any blobs or tails sticking up (these will make holes in the cake surface).

- Leave to dry thoroughly.

- Place the perspex icing-side down, on the top of a sugarpaste cake which has been left until the surface is no longer sticky.

- Press on the perspex firmly and evenly to emboss the pattern.

- Carefully remove and proceed with the embroidery.

LACE & FILIGREE

Lace has long been used decoratively on many garments and has been enthusiastically adopted by cake decorators to add a delicate finish to their fine work. Sometimes it is the main feature of a cake in the form of large filigree shapes.

Small lace pieces make a neat and dainty border when set above a band of extension work or frilling.

Several rows of lace, one above the other with fine bands of ribbon between, make an exquisite border and will require nothing more added to the side of a cake.

HINTS AND TIPS

- Freshly made Royal icing (preferably mixed by hand to medium peak) should be used. If it is to be coloured, liquid or diluted powder colours should be used in preference to paste colours as these often contain glycerol.

- A time-saving way of ensuring that the lace pieces are of uniform size, is to draw the chosen lace pattern and repeat it until you have a whole row. If the number in each row is kept to 10, it is easy to see at a glance how many pieces you have made.

- Small lace pieces look their best when very fine; a 00 or 0 tube will produce the best results. Since these tubes (tips) will easily clog, it is advisable to use special Bridal Icing Sugar when available or to sieve the sugar several times through a clean nylon stocking or fine sieve.

- Place the pattern under a piece of wax paper or non-stick film. Pipe over all the lines, ensuring that each line touches another line; any gaps will make weak spots and breakages may occur in these areas.

Dry very thoroughly before removing by sliding a fine-bladed palette knife under the lace.

Techniques

'MEXICAN HAT'

This term is widely used throughout the book and refers to a basic shape from which many flowers and sepals are cut.

Stages

1. Form a ball of flower paste into a cone.

2. Flatten the wider end of the cone between thumbs and fingers to form a flat disc.

3. Roll out from the centre with a paintbrush handle or small knitting needle until thin.

4. Using a hollow-centred cutter, cut out the shape of the flower.

5. Shape the petals with a ball tool.

HOLLOWING METHOD

Tools Required

- Small pointed scissors.

- Cocktail sticks (thin modelling sticks).

- Modelling tools – small & medium ball tools or dog bone tool, pointed tool.

- Small knitting needle (cable needle).

- Paintbrush, wires, fine stamens.

Stages *(see illustrations opposite)*

1. Roll a small ball of paste into a cone. If the paste has a tendency to stick to the hands or the modelling stick, use a little cornflour.

2. Hollow by inserting a cocktail stick. Rotate the cone against the side of the index finger with the stick inside until the walls are thin.

3. Cut the required number of petals with small pointed scissors.

4. Open out and trim off square corners.

5. Thin and improve petal shape by laying over a finger and rolling with a modelling stick – especially the edges.

6. Insert hooked wire and stamens. Finish each flower according to individual instructions.

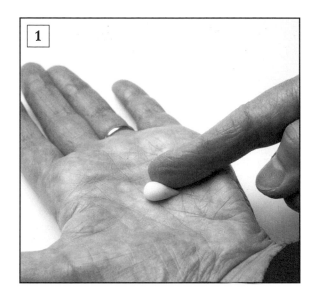

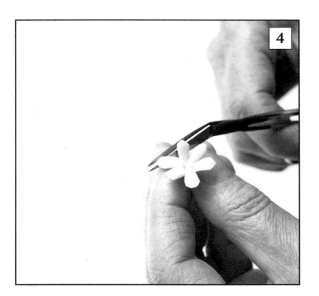

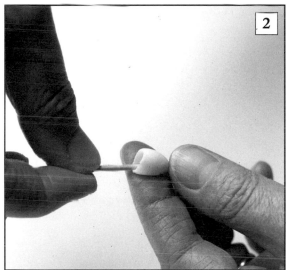

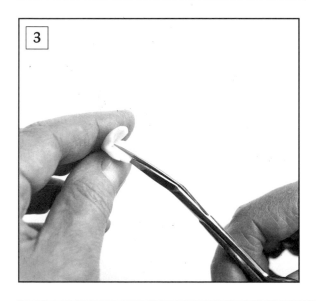

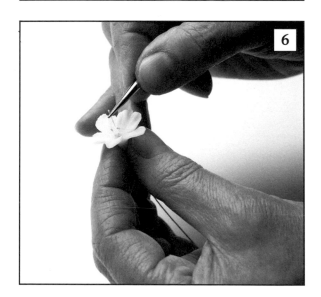

Leaves

These instructions are suitable for most wired leaves. Use different cutters/templates and veiners.

🍃 Roll out flower paste in an appropriate colour for the type of leaf (using a grooved rolling pin or board). Cut out leaf shape with the base of the cutter against a ridge.

🍃 Soften the edges of the leaf with a small ball tool and tool the centre, smoothing out the ridge except for about ½" (12 mm) at the base. Insert a piece of 26g. wire into the thickened area at the base of the leaf. Press the leaf on a veiner preferably made from a real leaf.

🍃 Pinch the leaf down the back of the central vein to give it some movement.

🍃 Dust the leaves with the colours found on a natural specimen, i.e. a darker green in the centre of a fresh green leaf; yellow, red and brown on Autumn leaves.

🍃 Glaze leaves with half-strength glaze for a fairly matt finish; three-quarter strength for glossy leaves.

See illustrations on opposite page ☞

BRUSH EMBROIDERY (*see page 27*)

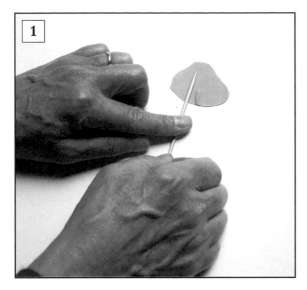

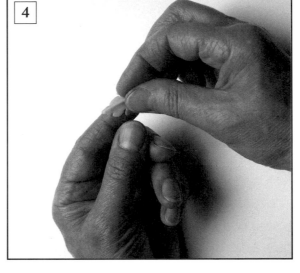

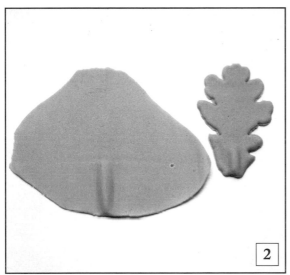

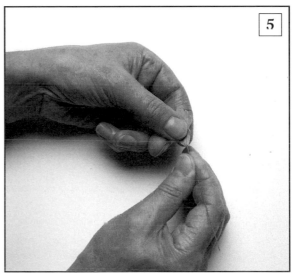

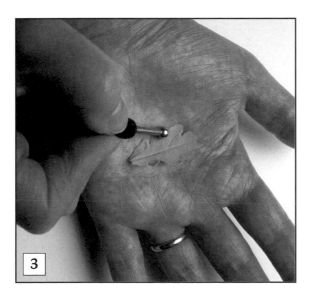

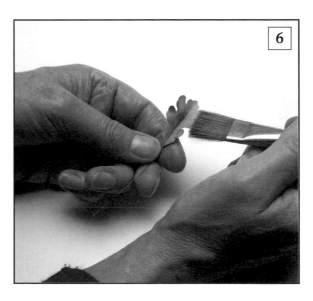

Singapore Orchid Cake

EQUIPMENT

12" (305mm) Round Board

Scriber

Scalpel

Icing Tubes (Tips) Nos 1 & 0

MATERIALS

8" (200mm) Round Cake

1 ½ lbs (750g) marzipan

1lb (500g) white sugarpaste plus

1lb extra if covering board

1 ½ lbs (750g) pale yellow paste

8ozs (250g) Royal Icing

Boiled sieved Apricot jam

Vodka

Brush the cake with boiled, sieved apricot jam. Cover the cake with marzipan. Leave until firm.

Brush the sides of the cake with Vodka. Make a template long enough to go all round the cake and wide enough to meet the curved edge at the top of the cake.

Cut a strip of white sugarpaste; carefully place the strip around the cake and join neatly. Smooth the sides and the top edge.

Cover the board with white icing and leave until firm. Cut out a circle from the centre to fit the cake. Place the cake in the centre of the board.

Roll out the yellow paste. Moisten the top of the cake only with Vodka. Lay the yellow icing over the cake, smooth the top and ease in the sides so there are no creases. Trim around the base.

Cut a thin paper template to fit around the sides of the cake. Fold the template into four equal sections and trace off the pattern (Dia. a.) including the curved line. Place around the cake and scribe the outline of the curve onto the cake. Using a sharp scalpel cut around the outline, releasing a curved section. Repeat around the cake.

With yellow icing and a N⁰. 0 tube (tip) pipe a picot edge around the cut out area.

With a N⁰. 1 tube (tip) and white icing pipe beading at the base of the cake.

Pipe the embroidered flower motif, using brush embroidery for the flowers and leaves; pipe bold stems with a N⁰. 1 tube.

Attach ribbon to the edge of the board.

Arrange a spray of Singapore Orchids, Freesias and Lily of the Valley. Attach to the top of the cake with a little icing or push into a posy holder.

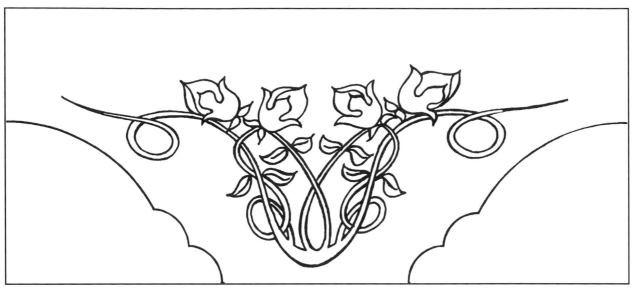

Side Panel Design (Dia. a). Trace four times onto the template. Adjust to fit if necessary by altering the length of the base line between the arches.

Picot Edge (detail, enlarged).

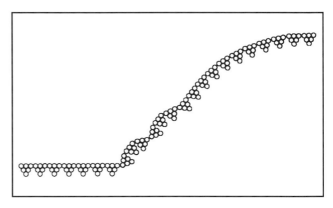

Picot Edge: repeat units around the edge of the paste.

Step by step

Top row (left to right):
former, sepals, shaped sepals.

Middle row:
petals, shaped petals, throat, shaped throat.

Lower row:
petals attached to sepals, completed flower, throat attached to column, column, bud.

Singapore Orchid *(Dendrobium)*

CUTTERS

Dendrobium Orchid Cutter

VEINERS

Corn on the Cob or Hibiscus

Sepals
Make one

Throat
Make one

Petal
Make two

- Make a former for the petals by cutting an empty drinks can in the shape of the sepals. Make a hole in the centre. Bend into a curved shape.
- Roll out thin white paste. Cut out the three sepals.
- Roll out more paste and cut out two petals. Soften edges and centre of the petals with a ball tool, vein lightly by pressing on a veiner.
- Mark a central vein on the front of each petal. Stick these two petals in between the sepals. Support the petals until dry with small pieces of foam.

Column

- Make a small cone of paste and stick onto a hooked 26g wire.
- Pinch a ridge either side of the cone and hollow underneath.
- Roll a tiny ball of pale yellow paste. Stick in the hollow of the column and mark a deep line in the middle with a veining tool.

Throat

- Cut out throat from thin white paste. Thin out the sides and the lip by rolling with a cocktail stick, press on a veiner. Attach the throat to the column, sticking with egg white or gum glue.
- Allow to dry. Push the wired throat through the hole in the petals and stick with glue. Allow to dry.
- Dust a little pale greenish yellow in the centre. Tape two more 24g wires against the stem to thicken it.

Bud

- Make a cone from a 10mm ball of paste. Roll the tail between thumb and finger into a slender point. Flatten the other end.
- Make two deep grooves in the back with a sharp knife. Bind three 24g wires together and insert into the middle of the bud. Curve both ends up.

Springtime

EQUIPMENT

14", 11",8" (355, 280, 200mm) round boards

Icing tubes (tips) Nos.1, 0, 00

Paper templates

MATERIALS

10", 8", 6" (255, 200, 150mm) round cakes

4½ lbs (2.25kg) marzipan

Boiled, sieved apricot jam

6½ lbs (3.25kg) champagne sugarpaste

8oz (250g) royal icing

Alcohol – gin or vodka

Food colouring (cream, brown)

FLOWER SPRAYS

Narcissi, Freesias, Periwinkle, Lily of the Valley, leaves, Catkins for top tier

Close up of flowers.

A bright and cheerful champagne wedding cake incorporating all the colours of Spring.

- Cut away a curved section from the large and medium cakes using **Template a** on page 18.

- Brush marzipanned cakes with boiled, sieved apricot jam. Cover all cakes with almond paste.

- Cover the boards with Regalice and leave to set for 1 – 2 days.

- Brush cakes with alcohol and cover with sugarpaste.

- Place the cakes in the centre of the covered boards and stick with a little boiled apricot jam.

Bottom and Middle Tier

- Cut paper templates to fit the sides of the cakes. Mark a line approximately 1"(25mm) from the base, curving to follow the shape of the high border at the front, on large and medium cakes (*see **Template b***). Prick the guideline from the template through to the cakes.

- Pipe embroidery in brown icing.

- Pipe neat beading around base of the cake with a N⁰· 1 icing tube (tip).

- Pipe bridgework on lower guideline with N⁰· 0 tube. Pipe extension work with N⁰· 0 or 00 tube from the upper guideline.

- Arrange flowers at board level, in the curve of the cake, set in a small cushion of sugarpaste.

Top Tier

- Pipe a straight band of extension work all around the base of the small cake.

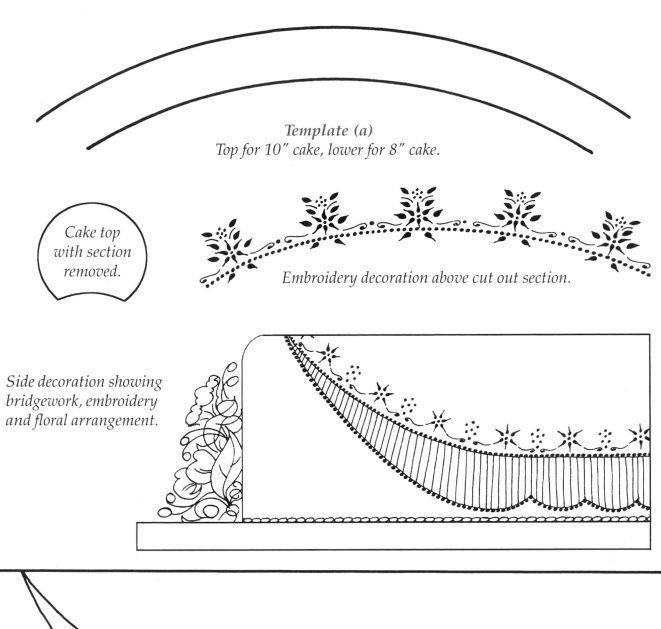

Template (a)
Top for 10" cake, lower for 8" cake.

Cake top with section removed.

Embroidery decoration above cut out section.

Side decoration showing bridgework, embroidery and floral arrangement.

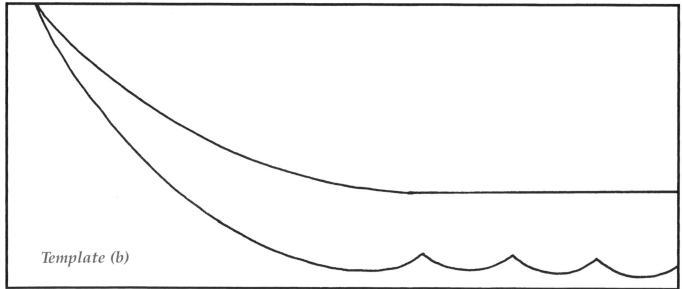

Template (b)

Narcissus

This flower is made by the 'hollowing method' without cutters. **(See below)**.

- Take a small ½" (12mm) ball of orange-coloured flower paste and roll it into a cone

- Hollow the cone by inserting a cocktail stick and rotate it until the sides of the cone are thin to form a trumpet shape.

- Texture the sides of the trumpet, by laying it on a piece of corn husk or similar veiner and press evenly from the inside. Frill the edges of the trumpet by rolling with a cocktail stick (rounded toothpick).

- Push a hooked 26g wire through the base of the trumpet. Insert six fine short stamens and one longer stamen in a tight bunch. Push them well down into the trumpet. Make another cone with cream coloured paste and hollow out as before.

- Cut out six petals by making two deep cuts on opposite sides of the cone, then cut each piece into three.

- Cut off the square corners. Shape the petals by rolling them with a cocktail stick.

- Insert the wired trumpet and stick with a little gum glue. Shape and thin the back by rolling between index fingers.

- Make a sheath by cutting out a thin, fine triangular piece of pale brown paste and stick to the back of the flower.

- Dust the edge of the trumpet with tangerine petal dust.

Decoration on top cake.

Narcissus Steps.

Periwinkle

🌿 Take a pea-sized ball of white paste and roll it into a cone. Hollow and widen (see **page 8**). Make five evenly-spaced deep cuts with a pair of small pointed scissors.

🌿 Snip off the square edges of the petals and trim at an angle so that the right side is slightly longer than the left.

🌿 Make a hole in the centre of the flower to form a throat by inserting a pointed tool with five ridges; the five points should be in the centre of each petal. The hole has five sides forming a pentagon. Press out each of the ridges until it is flat.

🌿 Thin the edges of the petals and slightly cup the centres with a dog bone tool. Insert a 28g hooked wire into the base and thin the back by rolling between fingers.

🌿 Place a yellow stamen in the centre to represent the stigma. The stamens are inside the petal tube and are not visible.

🌿 When dry, carefully dust the front and back of the petals with blue/violet dust, leaving a white centre. This can be made easier by masking the centre with a small plug of soft paste which can be removed after the dusting has been completed.

Calyx

Roll out pale green paste thinly, cut out shape with small star calyx cutter. Pinch the calyx points to narrow them. Slip over the wire and attach to the base of the flower with gum glue.

Buds

Roll a small ball of blue/violet paste, one quarter the size of that used for the flower, into a cigar shape. Roll the tip into a point. Insert wire into the base. Make lengthwise cuts in the bud, twist to spiral. Add a small calyx.

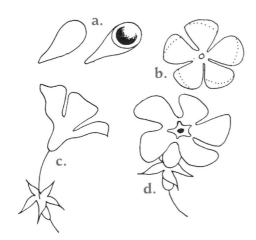

a. Hollowed cone.
b. Trim petals as dotted line.
c. Slide calyx onto base of flower.
d. Dust, leaving a white area in the centre.

Periwinkle flower.

Catkins

- Take a ¼" (6mm) ball of pale greenish-yellow paste. Moisten the end of a short length of sewing thread with egg white or gum glue

- Hold the thread next to the ball of paste and roll between thumb and finger to make a cigar shape about ¾" (18mm) long. The thread should now be inside the paste which should have taken the shape of a catkin.

- Insert a needle to make it easier to hold and texture by pinching with pointed metal tweezers. Allow to dry.

- Brush the catkin lightly with egg white and roll it in a small dish containing ground maize or semolina mixed with yellow petal dust, this will add the rough texture necessary to create the illusion of catkins covered with pollen. Make more catkins and leave to dry. Brush the stem end of some of the catkins with a little dark brown dust. If the green colour of the paste does not show through, stipple a little green in places.

- The catkins appear before the leaves and should be arranged in pairs.

- To make twigs take a piece of 24g wire. Make nodules by twisting the wire into knots at intervals. Bind it with brown stem tape to make a twig, pressing the tape around the knots neatly.

- Attach a pair of catkins to the end of the twig, binding in all of the thread and allowing them to hang freely.

- Bend the wire into a realistic twig shape, adding other twigs to make an attractive branch.

Arrangement of Catkins.

Texturing the catkin with tweezers.

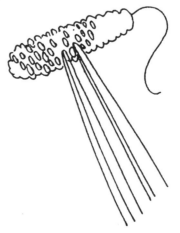

Magnolia

EQUIPMENT

14" x 12" (355x305mm) oval board

N⁰· 0 & 2 Paint Brushes

N⁰·1 & 2 Icing Tubes (tips)

1 yd. ¼" (5mm) satin ribbon

Paste Colours – violet, green, black

Paper Template

Magnolia Spray

Scriber

MATERIALS

11" x 9" (280x230mm) Scalloped Oval Cake

3 lbs (1.5kg) Marzipan

Boiled, sieved apricot jam

4 lbs (2kg) sugarpaste (rolled fondant)

8oz (250g) Royal Icing

Alcohol, Gin or Vodka

Method

❧ Knead a little violet colour into the sugarpaste (add a speck of black to give a softer, more subtle colour to the paste). Cover the board with thinly rolled paste. Cut out a section of paste in the centre, the same shape as the cake.

❧ Brush the cake with boiled, sieved apricot jam and cover with marzipan.

❧ Allow to set overnight.

❧ Brush the marzipan covering with alcohol. Roll out sugarpaste (rolled fondant) and cover the cake. Place the cake on the board, sticking with piping gel or jam.

❧ Allow the sugarpaste to harden for a few days before applying the pattern.

❧ Trace off the pattern of the Magnolias and enlarge on photocopier to fit the cake.

❧ Gently lay pattern on the cake, starting with the side pattern and arranging so that the side flowers are in the desired position. Using a scriber, draw over all lines to leave a fine guideline on the cake. Arrange the top template so that the pattern meets with the flowers on the side. Scribe through onto cake as before.

❧ Work Brush Embroidery as shown on *page 27.*

❧ Pipe fine beading around the base of the cake with pale mauve icing and a N⁰· 1 tube.

❧ Tape together a spray of Magnolias with buds and leaves. Either lay this loose on the cake or feed the wires into a posy holder before inserting into the cake.

Bare wires should never be pushed into cakes.

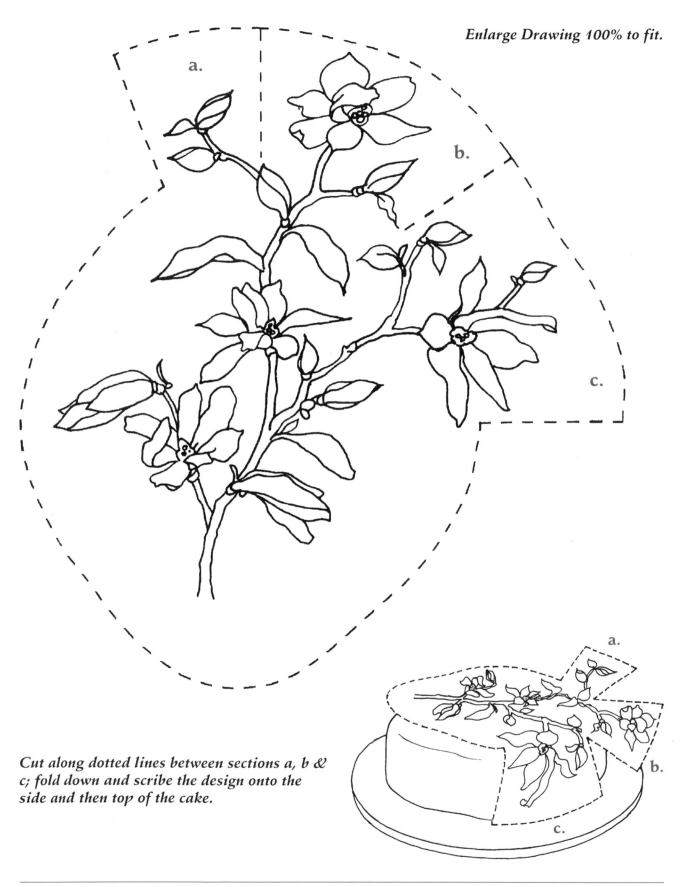

Enlarge Drawing 100% to fit.

a.

b.

c.

a.

b.

c.

Cut along dotted lines between sections a, b &
c; fold down and scribe the design onto the
side and then top of the cake.

Magnolia Flower

The Magnolia is a beautiful flower and with its delicate colouring makes an ideal cake decoration. As it is rather a large flower, the petals have been scaled down for this version to keep it in proportion with the cake.

Centre

- Roll a ball of pale green paste, about the size of a small pea, into a cone. Insert a piece of 26g covered wire into the base. Snip small points all over the cone with fine pointed scissors.

Stamens

- Cut out two daisy shapes from white paste. Cover one shape and snip the petals of the other into fine strands. Brush the daisy shape with egg white, slip over the wire and mould around the base of the centre. Repeat with second shape, slip onto the wire and mould around first layer of stamens. Paint stamen tips a deep mauvey-red.

Petals

- Roll out white paste thinly, leaving a thicker ridge at the base for the wire to be inserted.
- Cut 6 large petals and 3 smaller.
- While working on the first petal, cover the other petals with a plastic sheet to prevent them drying out.

> **CUTTERS**
>
> Magnolia , Small Daisy

- Thin the petal edges with a ball tool. Texture the petal with a suitable veiner. Make a central vein with a veining tool or by pinching down the middle of the petal, cup slightly and pinch the tip to a point.
- Insert an unhooked 30g white wire into the thickened ridge at the base. Repeat with all petals.
- The large petals should be curving towards the centre but the smaller outer petals may be curled back. Leave petals to dry.
- Dust the back of each petal delicately with a soft mauvey-pink, brushing from the base and gradually fading out.
- Tape the first three petals around the wired stamens, curving inwards. Add the next three, placing between the first row of petals. Finally, tape in the three smaller petals.

Closed Bud

- Make a green cone about 1½"(38mm) long. Insert a 26g hooked wire in the base. Cut 2 sections of calyx from Olive Green stemtape. Stick both sections to the base of the bud *(see diagram on* **page 26***)*.

Opening Bud

- Make white cone about 1½" (38mm) long. Insert hooked wire into base. Cut three petals (unwired); shape and stick around cone with egg white or gum glue. Add Stemtape calyx.
- Roll a little pale green paste around the stem at the base of all flowers and buds. Pinch ridges around the stem.

Magnolia Steps

Top Row *(from left to right)*: *Centre, Wired centre, Stamens (Daisy shape), Stamens (snipped finely), Complete centre, Petal, Cut petal, Shaped petal.*

Lower Row: *Petals arranged around centre, Finished flower.*

Stemtape Calyx

1. Two overlapping pieces of stemtape.

2. Stretch to release glue.

3. Mark out Calyx shape.

4. Cut out Calyx (make two).

5. Cup the two pieces of the Calyx and attach to the base of bud opposite each other.

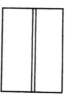 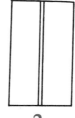 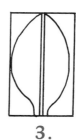  

1.   2.   3.   4.   5.

Brush Embroidery. (Close-up).

Brush Embroidery

This versatile cake decorating technique is simply a method of painting in icing and a means of producing attractive designs quickly and easily.

The design can be worked in white or cream on a dark background, in which case the decorator will use brush strokes to emphasise the veining of leaves and the textures of the petals.

Colour may be introduced either by using coloured icing, by using white icing but adding a little colour to the brush when brushing through, or by completing the picture in pale colours and highlighting with a little colour when the work is completely dry.

Materials

❧ A N⁰ 0 tube (tip) should be used when the design is very small, but normally a N⁰ 1 is used. Use a good quality brush with plenty of spring in it; a N⁰ 2 or 3 for brushing the icing and adding colour highlights; a 0 or 00 brush for adding fine detail.

❧ A soft peak icing should be used and the addition of a small amount of piping gel will give a longer working time.

Method

❧ Allow the icing of the cake to set for a few days before transferring the design by pricking through the pattern onto the cake.

❧ Half fill small piping bags containing the correct size tube (tip).

❧ Start working from the outside of the design towards the centre. Deal with all the background first and keep the texture of the icing thin at this stage.

❧ As you work towards the front of the design, the pressure on the icing tube may be increased to make the foreground bolder.

❧ Using a damp paintbrush, flatten the bristles like a spade for stroking the icing. Pipe a line around the first leaf or petal. Pipe a heavier line at the tip of the petal and brush the icing through with long strokes towards the base of the petal *(see diagrams below)*. Always brush in a continuous line from tip to base for petals; the slightly damp brush will produce texturing. Leaves should be brushed diagonally from the tip to the centre on each side; the final brush stroke through the centre of the leaf will emphasise the central vein.

❧ Details like stamens and any other features which require to be emphasised should be carefully piped in with a fine tube. Shadows and highlights may be added when the work is completely dry, using a fairly dry brush and dilute colour.

White embroidery on a white background.

❧ This makes an excellent decoration for a wedding cake where delicacy is required. Contrasts of light and shadow play a big part in making this type of design visible, therefore the contours must be well-defined by using more pressure than usual (for example see Clematis Cake). The tips of the petals should be given extra emphasis by piping quite a thick line, the petal is then brushed from this line to the base. When it is finished there should be a heavy rim, graduating to a thin wash at the base.

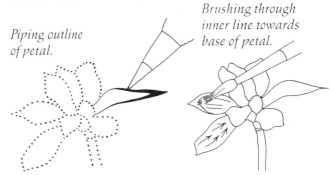

Piping outline of petal.

Brushing through inner line towards base of petal.

Fuchsia Cake

EQUIPMENT

11" (280mm) round board

Nos. 0 & 1 Icing tube (tip)

Parchment paper template

Thin card template

Scalpel

Scriber

MATERIALS

8" (200mm) round cake

Boiled sieved apricot jam

Vodka or other alcohol

1 ½ lbs (750g) Marzipan

1 ½ lbs (750g) Aubergine colour Sugarpaste for board and cake sides

1 lb (500g) Pink sugarpaste for top

A two-tone cake in aubergine and pale pink, designed to blend with the colours of the Fuchsias on the top of the cake. The pink top is textured by 'ragging' with claret colouring diluted with water.

Aubergine colour – Claret with a little black (a lot of paste colour will be required to achieve this strong shade).*

- Brush the cake with boiled, sieved apricot jam. Cover with marzipan. Allow to dry overnight. Cover the board with sugarpaste and cut away an 8" (200mm) circle in the centre using the cake tin as a guide.

- Make a paper template to fit the sides of the cake and use it to cut a strip of aubergine coloured paste. Brush the sides of the cake with alcohol and apply the strip of aubergine coloured paste to the sides of the cake, smoothing the top edge so that there is no ridge. Place the cake on the board and leave until the icing is set.

- Brush the top of the cake with alcohol, leaving the sides dry.

- Roll out the pink paste and drape this over the cake. Smooth the top and mould the paste around the sides.

- Make another template to fit around the sides of the cake. Fold into four sections.

- Draw pattern of side curve onto the template *(Dia. a)*. Repeat on all four sections. Replace the template around the cake and mark the curved line on the cake with a scriber.

- Cut out a template of the curved shape in thin card.

- Place this template against the scribed line and cut around it with a sharp scalpel. Repeat all around the cake, allowing the surplus paste to fall away. Smooth the cut edges carefully with a finger.

- Pipe beading around the base of the cake with a N⁰ 1 tube (tip) and pale pink icing. Mark a line ½" (12mm) inside the outer edge of the board. Pipe fine embroidery with a N⁰ 0 tube tip.

- Mark a line ½" above the cut edge of the pink overlay. Pipe a fine embroidered line with a N⁰ 0 tube and aubergine coloured icing.

- Pipe small lace pieces on non-stick film and allow to dry. Attach to the edge of the overlay with small dots of icing. Arrange Fuchsias with leaves and buds in a posy holder.

* N.B. When overlaying a dark colour, care should be taken to cover this area of the cake so that it does not get marked. Place a collar of greaseproof paper around the base of the cake to protect the board by cutting a hole the size of the cake and slipping it over the cake until it rests on the board. The sides of the cake may be similarly protected with a collar of paper which may be removed when the overlay is completed.

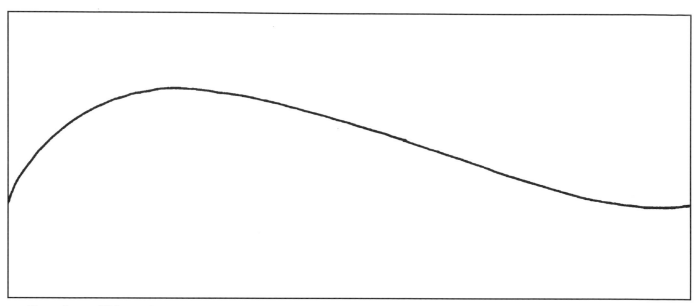

Template. (Dia. a.).

Embroidery pattern on the board.   *Lace piece.*   *Embroidery pattern on the cake.*

Close-up of flowers on cake.   *Side of cake showing embroidery.*

Fuchsia Flower

Tape nine stamens to a half-length 24g wire, leaving one longer than the others. The stamens differ in colour according to the main flower colour.

Petals

Roll out paste very thinly and cut out two shapes with cutter **b**. Slightly flute the tips of the petals by rolling with a cocktail stick. Cup each petal by working with a ball tool. Moisten the centre with gum glue and push the wired stamens through. Cup the petals around the stamens arranging them evenly and encourage them to curl at the edges. Repeat with the second set of petals. Draw up over the first row and arrange neatly.

Calyx

Make a Mexican hat shape *(see **page 8**)* with paste of a contrasting colour. Cut out calyx with Cutter **a**. Thin out the sepals, particularly the edges with a ball tool. Open up the centre by inserting a pointed tool. Place the calyx upside down on a piece of foam. Curl up the sepals by stroking from the tip to the centre with a ball tool. Brush the hollowed centre with gum glue and insert the wired petals. Roll the back of the calyx between two fingers to thin it. Remove any excess paste.

Make the ovary by rolling a very small ball of green paste into a cone, flatten the wide end of the cone and attach this neatly to the base of the calyx.

Buds

Make some small green buds and some larger ones the same colour as the calyx. Roll a ball of paste, point the tip and thin out the base. Cut four lengthwise ridges down the bud. Add the ovary as for the flower. Tape together flowers, leaves *(see **page 10**)* and buds in a natural arrangement.

EQUIPMENT

Fuchsia Cutters

Fuchsia Cutters

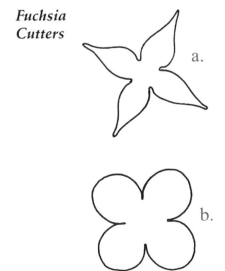

a.

b.

Wild Rose

EQUIPMENT

14",11",8" (355, 280, 200mm) round boards

Icing tubes (tips) 00 or 0, 1,2

Wax paper

Paintbrushes

Scriber

Briar Roses, leaves and Speedwell

MATERIALS

10 ", 8", 6" (250, 200, 150mm) round cakes

4 ½ lbs (2.25kg) Marzipan

6 ½ lbs (3.25kg) Sugarpaste

Royal Icing without glycerine

Piping gel

Food colours – pink and green

Boiled sieved apricot jam

The basic design for this cake follows a diagonal line which sweeps down the side of the cake from a point at the centre to a wide band at the base. This is repeated on the other side of the cake so that an identical design can be seen from both sides. The direction of the line goes the opposite way on alternate cakes and the complete design follows the lines of the spiral cake stand.

❧ Cover the cake boards with sugarpaste and leave to set firm.

❧ Cut a circle of paste from the centre of each board, using the cake tin as a guide.

❧ Brush cakes with boiled, sieved apricot jam and cover with marzipan. Leave overnight. Cover cakes with sugarpaste and place on the boards. Allow to set for a few days.

❧ Make side templates for each size of cake. Make top templates. *(See Pages 34/35)*

❧ Place side templates around the cake and secure with masking tape. Scribe the pattern through onto the cake. Lay top template on the cake, matching up border lines. Scribe through pattern.

❧ Pipe beading around the base of each cake.

❧ Make lace by placing a piece of non-stick film or wax paper over the pattern and piping with N° 0 or 00 tube (tip). Allow to dry thoroughly.

❧ Add piping gel to some of the Royal icing and work the rose and leaf pattern in Brush Embroidery, starting with the background leaves on the top and sides of each cake *(See **Brush Embroidery** – Page 27).*

❧ Attach lace pieces neatly along border lines with small dots of icing.

❧ Make Briar Roses, leaves and Speedwell. Attach small clusters of flowers and leaves to the board at the base of the floral bands, both sides of the cake.

❧ The top ornament is formed by making an 'arch' with several strands of white covered wire taped together. The ends are inserted into a cushion of modelling paste. Flowers and leaves are inserted into the base before it dries and more small flowers and tiny leaves are arranged trailing around the arch. A similar ornament can be made by decorating a purchased cake top ornament.

Template for top of bottom Tier.

This edge on rim of cake.

This point in centre of cake.

This edge on rim of cake

Template for side of bottom tier.

This point in centre of cake.

Template for top tier.
(Side only).

*This edge
on rim of
cake.*

**Template
for top of
middle
tier.**

These edges on rim of cake.

Template for side of middle tier.

Close-up of Brush Embroidery.

Briar Rose

The cotton stamens

🌿 Wind cream or pale yellow sewing thread around two fingers until you have enough for the flower which does have many stamens. Remove the circle of cotton from your fingers and insert a length of fine wire through the loop, bringing the ends together and giving a firm twist to secure the threads. Cut through the threads, leaving them approximately ½" (12mm) long. Bring all the threads together and tape them at the base with ¼" (5mm) width florists tape to stop them separating. Continue taping the wires together. Spread the threads to find the centre.

🌿 Make a tiny cone with pale green paste. Dab a little egg white or glue into the middle of the threads and push the small centre into it. Brush the tips of the threads with egg white and dip into pollen (made by adding yellow petal dust to cornmeal or semolina). Separate the threads if necessary and leave to dry. For the mature rose dab the tips of the stamens with flecks of dark brown.

The Calyx

🌿 Make a Mexican Hat from a small piece of mid-green paste. Cut out shape with a medium calyx cutter. Snip the sides of the sepals with small pointed scissors. Thin out the tips of the sepals by stroking with a dog bone tool. Cup the centre of the calyx slightly. Put on one side.

Petals

🌿 Cut out five petals with a Dog Rose cutter. Thin the edges of the petals with a ball tool and cup the centre. Texture the petals by pressing gently on a fine veiner.

🌿 Brush the calyx with egg white and arrange the petals evenly with the points to the centre (see Dia., **page 38**). Press firmly into position and push the wired stamens through the centre of the rose. Adjust the petals to form a pleasing shape.

🌿 Roll the base of the calyx between fingers to form the shape of the ovary.

🌿 Strengthen the stem by adding a 24g wire and taping it to the existing fine wires.

Bud

🌿 Refer to instructions for Quick Rose (see **page 70**). Follow instructions for the first layer of petals. Make Calyx as above and bring the sepals up to cup the bud.

Leaves

🌿 Make the leaves following general instructions as described on pages **10 & 11**.

🌿 Tape groups of five leaves together.

Lace Pattern.

Positions for petals and leaves.

Dog Rose. (calyx, petal, leaf.)

Wild Rose.

Rose. Step by Step.

Speedwell

The Flower

🌿 Take a 5mm ball of blue paste, roll it into a cone and hollow with a cocktail stick *(see **Hollowing Method, page 8**)*. Cut one narrow petal from the edge of the cylinder with small pointed scissors. Open out the remainder of the edge and cut into three equal parts. Cut off the corners to make rounded petals. Thin the edges of the petals by stroking with a dog bone tool.

🌿 Make a small hook in a piece of 28g wire. Push through the centre of the flower. Neaten the back.

🌿 Place a tiny ball of white paste in the centre of the petals. Push firmly with the end of a cocktail stick, making a small round hole, this makes the white 'eye'. Insert two fine brown tipped stamens protruding beyond the flower and facing in opposite directions, right and left. Insert one short green stamen in between for the stigma.

🌿 Paint very fine dark blue veins from the centre of each petal, radiating towards the tip.

Calyx

🌿 Roll a small ball of pale green paste (2mm) into a cone. Cut in two halves with small scissors then cut each half into two again, making four lobes. Pinch flat between thumb and finger then pinch into points. Slide calyx along the wire and attach to the base of the flower.

Clematis Cascade

EQUIPMENT

16", 12", 9" (405, 305, 230mm) boards

3 Posy Holders

Icing Tubes (tips) Nos. 1 & 0

Parchment icing bags

Paint Brushes Nos. 2 & 3

Scriber

Paper Templates

Green and brown stemtape

Board Ribbon – 10mm wide

Narrow Ribbon – 5mm wide

4 tier adjustable offset cakestand or 3 tier stand and pedestal

flower holder

MATERIALS

12", 9", 7" (305, 230, 180mm) rich fruit cakes

Apricot jam – boiled and sieved

6 lbs (3kg) Marzipan

Clear alcohol (Gin or Vodka)

9 lbs (4.5kg) Sugarpaste (rolled fondant)

Small amount Royal Icing

Icing Sugar (Confectioner's) for rolling out

8 large Clematis Jackmanii

6 Pink Clematis Montana

6 Stems Summer Jasmine

8 Sprays Clematis leaves & 4 Ivy

BOUQUET

9 Large Purple Clematis

5 Pink Clematis Montana.

6 Sprays Summer Jasmine

10 Sprays Clematis leaves

4 Ivy sprays

An unusual Wedding Cake decorated with sprays of richly coloured Clematis, making a bold contrast with the pure white embroidery on the cakes. The pattern of the embroidery was taken from a piece of embroidered lace. The separate arrangement of sugar flowers compliments the flowers on the cakes. It may be arranged in a separate tall flower vase or by removing the disc from one of the hollow supports of a 4-tier Offset Cakestand and arranging the spray in the top of the the hollow support.

- Brush the cakes with boiled, sieved apricot jam. Cover with marzipan and leave overnight for the surface to dry.

- Cover the cake boards with sugarpaste and leave until firm. Cut away a circle the size of the cake in the centre of each board.

- Brush the cakes with Vodka and cover with sugarpaste. Place in position on the board. Allow the covering to dry for several days until firm before applying the pattern with a scriber.

- Trace the pattern and lay it in position on the top of the cake. Scribe or prick out the details of the design. If you wish to use the embossing method, this should be done while the icing is still soft *(see **page 7**)*.

- Pipe neat beading around the base of the cakes with a N$^{\circ}$ 1 tube (tip).

- Using white icing and a N$^{\circ}$ 1 tube (tip) work the pattern in brush embroidery, using extra pressure to give a well-defined design.

- Place a band of thin ribbon around the cake at board level.

- Insert a posy holder into the base of each cake, fill with soft sugarpaste and arrange flowers and leaves by inserting the wires into the holder; the paste will hold them in position. The larger spray on the bottom tier will require two posy holders.

The large bouquet

- The bouquet is composed of large and small Clematis flowers, Ivy leaves, clematis leaves, with a few sprigs of Jasmine. To achieve the loose natural arrangement long stems should be used, half the length of a standard piece of covered wire.

- Tape together two long Ivy trails. Add one purple Clematis, taped together with two leaves and one bud; one spray of leaves to the left and one spray of pink Clematis Montana with leaves to the right.

- Carry on adding flowers and sprays of leaves so that there is a cluster of flowers in the centre with the leaves forming a frame around them. Follow the photograph for more details of the arrangement.

This pattern fits the top tier.
Please enlarge to fit the middle
and bottom tiers.

This unit fits the top tier. Please enlarge to
fit the middle and bottom tiers. The units
are repeated around the top of the cakes.

Clematis Steps *(right)*

From left, anti-clockwise:

Petals

Stamens

Centre

Centre with stamens

Half assembled flower

Complete flower.

Large Spray.

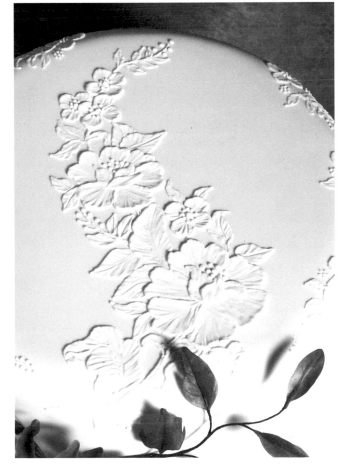

Close-up of Cake top.

Clematis

This trailing shrub makes a charming cake decoration, particularly for tiered cakes. The many different varieties range from small four petal flowers to large showy flowers with six, seven or eight petals . The wide range of colours also make this very appealing to cake decorators who should have no trouble incorporating the Clematis into many colour schemes.

Stamens (paste)

🍂 Make the centre by taking a small (5mm) ball of pale green paste, insert a 26g. wire.

🍂 Roll out white flower paste very thinly. Cut out two shapes with a small Daisy cutter. Shred each petal by making a series of fine snips down the length of the petals. Brush the centre with 'glue'. Mould the first 'Daisy' shape, cupping the stamens around the centre. Attach the second layer and fan the stamens out. Paint the tips with a mixture of violet and black colour.

For correct colouring of different varieties refer to the individual flower. Paint fine purple or black lines on centre, like spokes of a wheel; these represent closed stamens.

Petals

🍂 Thinly roll out paste for petals, using a ridged roller or board. Cut out the required number of petals with the thickened ridge at the base using cutter or template *(Dia.a)*. While working on the first petal, keep the remainder covered with plastic film.

🍂 Press petal against a special veiner, or mark centre veins with a veining tool. Flute the edge of the petal with a small ball tool or gently frill with a cocktail stick (toothpick). Insert a piece of white covered 28g wire into the thickened ridge at the base of the petal. Pinch the back of the petal to emphasise the central vein. Twist petals into a natural shape and leave to dry.

Assembly

🍂 Bend the petals at an angle of 45° from the wire. Arrange the petals evenly around the central stamens and tape into position.

Leaves

🍂 Follow basic instructions on pages *10* and *11*.

🍂 Clematis leaves vary a lot in size and shape. The template *(Dia.c)* shows a typical leaf shape. Cutters are now available.

Clematis *Montana*

🍂 Make a centre the same as for *Jackmanii* but using pale yellow paste.

🍂 Roll out white or pale pink paste and cut out four petals using the small size Clematis cutter *(Dia. b)*. Press petals on a veiner, soften the edges with a ball tool. Pinch the back of the petal along the central vein. Insert lengths of white wire into the base of the petals. Allow to dry in a natural shape.

🍂 Dust the edges of the petals with pale pink petal dust.

🍂 Bend the petals to an angle of 45° and tape them around the centre. Bend the petals into an attractive shape.

🍂 Tape four petals evenly around the centre.

CUTTERS

Clematis (2 sizes), Small Daisy, Clematis Leaf

VEINERS

Clematis or Lily, Clematis leaf, Clematis Jackmanii

Summer Jasmine

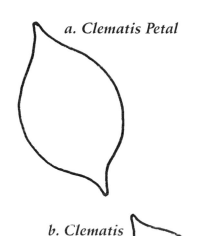

a. Clematis Petal

b. Clematis Petal

c. Clematis Leaf

Stephanotis Cutter.

Flower

🌫 Make a cone of white paste *(See **Mexican Hat,** page 8)*. Flatten the broad end and roll thin with a small knitting needle (cable needle). Cut out flower shape.

🌫 Soften the edges of the petals with a dog bone tool. Moisten the tip of a 28g wire and pull it through the flower. Roll the back of the flower between fingers to thin and taper. Hollow the centre of the flower with a fine pointed tool.

🌫 Insert one short stamen into the centre of the flower.

Bud

🌫 Roll a very small ball of paste into a cigar shape, taper one end by rolling between fingers. Shape the bulbous end to a point. Insert a 28g wire into the narrow end of the tube.

🌫 Dust the buds and the backs of the flowers pale pink.

🌫 Arrange clusters of buds and petals.

Spray of Jasmine.

Autumn Tints

EQUIPMENT

14", 9" (355,230mm) round boards

Paint brushes

N°· 0 & 1 tubes (tips)

Scriber

MATERIALS

10", 7" (255,180mm) round cakes

3 ½ lbs (1.75kg) Marzipan

Boiled sieved apricot jam

Alcohol (Gin or Vodka)

5 lbs (2.5kg) Champagne Sugarpaste

8 ozs (250g) Royal Icing

Single Chrysanthemums, Oats & Rose Hips

2 sprays Autumn Leaves & White Bryony

The colours of the single Chrysanthemums , berries and leaves blend well to make this an ideal cake for an Autumn wedding or Anniversary. The Chrysanthemums are made in the same way as the Ox-eye Daisy; the colour can be white, yellow, russet-red or orange and the centres are usually a greenish/yellow.

❧ Cover the boards with Sugarpaste (Rolled Fondant). Cut away a section of paste in the centre, using the cake tin as a guide.

❧ Brush cakes with boiled, sieved apricot jam. Cover with marzipan.

❧ Allow to dry overnight. Brush the cakes with alcohol and cover with sugarpaste (rolled fondant).

❧ Place the cakes in position on the boards, sticking with jam. Leave to set for a few days. Trace floral pattern onto a template. Attach to the cake and scribe the design onto the side of the cake.

❧ Pipe neat beading around the base of the cakes.

❧ (It is less confusing if you scribe the main lines of the pattern onto the cake and pipe the remainder of the design freehand).

❧ The pattern is worked with a N°· 0 tube (tip) in tube embroidery which is similar to the sewing technique .

❧ To work this type of embroidery, use the tip of the icing tube as you would draw with a pencil. The only difference is that you will be gently squeezing icing from the bag while piping the design. Small designs should be piped in outline only whereas slightly larger petals may be filled in by piping short lines ('stitches') close together in the form of a zig -zag pattern as in machine embroidery. Emphasis may be put on certain areas by squeezing the icing bag more firmly to build up a bulb of icing before dragging the tube in the direction of the pattern.

❧ Make Chrysanthemums in different shades; a variety of Autumn leaves, sprays of Oats, White Bryony and Rosehips, following directions given.

❧ Tape together berries, leaves and flowers. Arrange loose flowing sprays, trailing over the sides of the cakes.

❧ The wires should be inserted into a cushion of sugarpaste or a posy pick-(two posy picks will be required for the large spray). Support in the required position until set.

Do not allow wires to come into direct contact with the cakes.

Tube Embroidery

Bottom tier: Fold template into 6. Trace & Scribe the design 5 times around the cake and in the space of the 6th panel place the floral arrangement.

Top tier: Fold template into 4. Trace & scribe the design 4 times around the cake.

Close up of floral arrangement on bottom tier.

Chrysanthemum/Ox-Eye Daisy

Both flowers are made by the same method. For the Daisy use white paste for the petals, golden yellow for the centre. The Chrysanthemum may have a pale green centre. Petals yellow, white, orange, rusty red or pink.

The Flower

ᚙ Make a Mexican hat shape *(see **page 8**)* with a pea-sized ball of paste in your chosen colour.

ᚙ Cut out the petals with a large Daisy cutter. Cut each petal in half lengthwise with small scissors. Place the flower face down on a board and roll the cocktail stick back and forth to thin the petals. Press a ball tool into the centre to make a slight hollow.

ᚙ Insert a hooked piece of 26g wire into the base of the flower. Neaten the back by rolling it in between your fingers. Keep the back short as this is a fairly flat flower.

ᚙ Roll out paste very thinly, cut another Daisy shape, this time flat. Cut each petal in half and roll with a cocktail stick as for the first petals.

ᚙ Brush the centre of the first row of petals with gum glue. Lay the second layer centrally on top.

ᚙ Make a yellow or green centre by pressing a small ball of paste into a piece of fine mesh to texture it. If you press well into the mesh, the paste will take on the appearance of a mass of tiny florets. Moisten the middle of the Daisy petals with gum glue and press the centre into the hollow. Moisten the centre with a little gum glue and dust with cornmeal or fine semolina, mixed with yellow/green petal dust, to make pollen. Gently tease the petals into a natural random formation.

> ### CUTTERS
> Large size Daisy cutter and smallest Daisy cutter

The Calyx

ᚙ Roll out some mid-green paste. Cut out two shapes with a small Daisy cutter. Cut each lobe in half lengthwise. Thin the points.

ᚙ Brush the base of the flower with gum glue. Slide the bracts over the wire and stick to the base of the flower. Attach a second row of bracts, arranged below the first row.

Ox-Eye Daisy. Steps.

Finished flowers.

Chrysanthemum.
Step by step.

Oats

- Make a hook in the end of a piece of 30g wire. Mould a tiny ball of cream coloured paste around the hook. Press to flatten.

- Roll out paste thinly and cut out two petals. Thin the edges and cup the centre of both petals with a small ball tool. Brush the base of both petals with egg white and attach them opposite to each other on the wire.

- The petals should be open and bearing in mind that they would have just released a seed vary the way that you curve them.

- Tape the wire with one-third width of white flower tape and dust it a creamy-brown colour.

CUTTER

Small leaf or sepal of mini Orchid

White Bryony

CUTTERS

Small Calyx Cutter

Bryony leaf cutter or template.

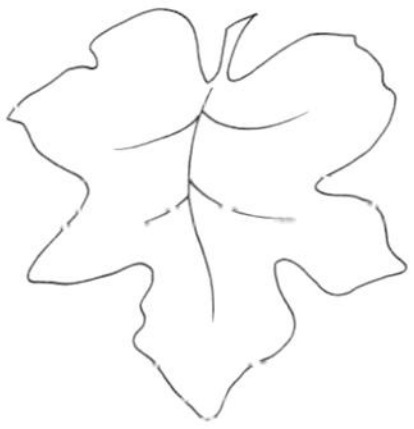

Bryony leaf.

Small Calyx Cutter.

Bryony leaf, buds and flowers.

Flowers

❧ Make a Mexican hat shape *(see **page 8**)* with very pale green paste. Cut out the flower with a small five-pointed calyx cutter. Thin the edges of the petals with a small ball tool. Make a hollow in the centre of the flower with a narrow pointed tool. Insert a hooked 30g wire. Neaten the back of the flower which should be small and dainty.

❧ The Buds are small and flat with five sections.

Leaves

❧ Roll out pale green paste using a grooved rolling pin or board. Cut out leaf shape. Soften the edges of the leaf with a small ball tool. Insert a piece of 26g. wire into the thickened area at the base of the leaf. Press leaf on a veiner preferably made from a real leaf. Pinch the leaf down the back of the central vein. Dust lightly down the centre of the leaf with dark green petal dust (green & black mixed). Glaze with half-strength glaze *(see **Recipes**, page 6)*.

❧ Make a trail of flowers, buds and leaves as shown in the picture. Add curly tendrils made by curling very fine covered green wire around a cocktail stick (toothpick).

Honeysuckle

Flowers

❧ Tape five very fine short stamens and one long one (for the stigma) to a piece of 30g wire.

❧ Roll a ball of paste about ¼" (6mm) into a cigar shape. Push a cocktail stick into one end until it is about half way down the tube. Hollow *(see **Hollowing Method**, page 8).*

❧ With small pointed scissors make two long cuts very close together to make a long narrow petal. Pull this petal gently forward to separate it from the remainder.

❧ Open out the rest of the cylinder and cut a deep wedge from either side to make more space between the long petal and the rest of the petals. Cut three small V's along the top of this broad lip, forming four lobes. Pinch between thumb and finger and gently curl back.

❧ Trim the square corners from the narrow petal. Pinch and gently curve down towards the base.

Push wired stamens through the throat and out of the bottom of the long tube. Roll the base between fingers to taper well.

Buds

❧ Roll a smaller piece of paste into a long tapering cone. Push the wire into the base, taper the tip and narrow the base. Curve slightly over the pad of a thumb. Dust the base of the flowers and buds with pale orangey-pink.

❧ Assemble buds and flowers with a cluster of buds in the centre, surrounded by flowers. The flowers should lie at 90° to the centre with the long narrow petal facing downwards.

❧ The sepals of these flowers are very small and joined at the base. These can be represented by pressing tiny balls of green paste in between the bases of all flowers and buds, moulding into shape with a modelling tool.

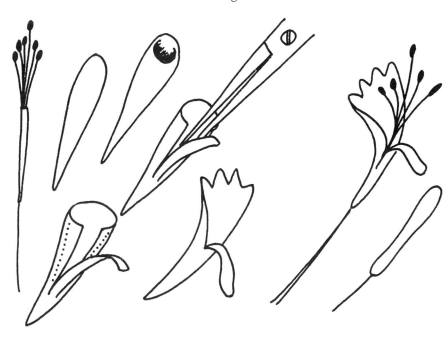

Honeysuckle,
step by step.

Honeysuckle Spray.

Rose Hip

These Rose Hips are made smaller than life-size to blend well into an Autumn arrangement.

❧ Roll a pea-sized ball of orangey-red paste into a cone-shape. Insert a hooked 28g wire into the wide base.

❧ Cut a small calyx from thinly rolled brownish-green paste Thin the sepals with a small ball tool until they look 'papery'.

❧ Brush the point of the hip with egg white and attach the calyx, pressing it down well and curling up the sepals.

❧ Dust the hip with red and brush with glaze, avoiding the calyx which does not have a gloss.

Daisy

EQUIPMENT

12" (305mm) Hexagon board

¾ yd (700 mm) ribbon (5mm wide)

Smocking Kit

Garrett Frill Cutter

Scriber

Icing tubes 0 & 1

Small Daisy Cutter

Card template

Moulded arrangement of daises & Ivy leaved Toadflax

MATERIALS

8" (200mm) Hexagonal cake

1½ lbs (750g) Marzipan

Boiled sieved Apricot jam

1½ lbs (750g) Sugarpaste

1 lb (500g) Sugarpaste for board.

Small quantity Royal Icing

Vodka or other spirit

8oz (250g) Smocking paste

This pretty hexagonal cake would be equally appropriate for a christening cake or a young person's birthday. Smocking panels are applied to form petals around the top edge. Smocking kits (including instructions) available from good sugarcraft shops.

❧ Brush the cake with boiled, sieved apricot jam. Cover with marzipan. Cover the board with sugarpaste. Cut out an 8" (200mm) hexagon of paste from the centre, using the cake tin as a guide. Brush the cake with Vodka and cover with sugarpaste. Place in the centre of the board. Pipe beading around the base with a N⁰· 1 tube (tip).

❧ Mark a 6" (150mm) circle in the centre of the cake with a scriber. Trace the **Smocking Template** and cut out the shape in thin card.

❧ Roll out the Smocking paste 3mm thick on cornflour with a plain roller **(Dia. 1)**.

❧ With a smocking roller lightly dusted with cornflour, roll firmly over the paste from the bottom edge to produce the ridged effect **(Dia. 2)** [do not allow the paste to stick to your board]. Place the Template on the ridged paste and cut around it with a sharp knife *(see template, p.56)* [A pizza wheel is useful for this will not drag the paste out of shape]. Cut six panels.

❧ When completed brush the back of each ridged section with a little alcohol and apply to the cake centrally between the points of the hexagon with the inner edge against the circular guideline.

❧ Join the ridged sections neatly, easing them if necessary to form a neat seam.

❧ Mark a honeycombe smocking pattern with tweezers **(Dia. 4)**.

❧ Pipe embroidery in a contrasting colour **(Dia. 5)**.

❧ Make a narrow frill and attach it to the edge of the smocking with a little water. Pipe a neat line of beading where the frill joins the smocking.

❧ Attach a narrow ribbon neatly along the join, with icing, between the smocked pieces. Make neat bows and attach them to each point on the cake at the end of the ribbon.

❧ Cut out small Daisy shapes. Press into a piece of foam to cup them. Attach the Daisies to the inner circle with dots of icing. Pipe little yellow dots in the centre of each flower.

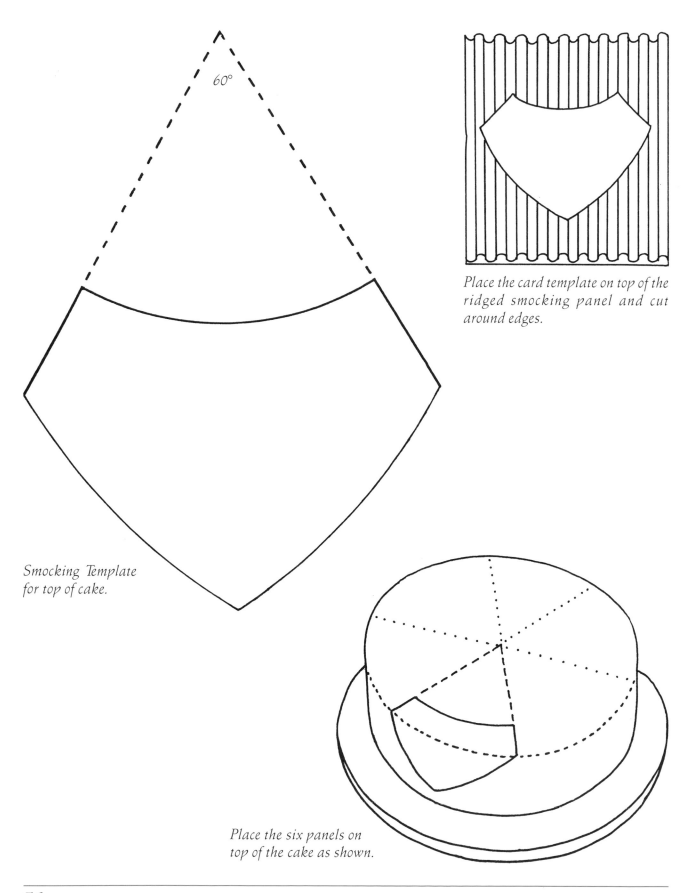

60°

Smocking Template
for top of cake.

Place the card template on top of the
ridged smocking panel and cut
around edges.

Place the six panels on
top of the cake as shown.

1. *Roll out paste 3mm thick with a plain roller.*

2. *Roll over again with grooved roller to obtain ribbed effect.*

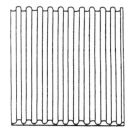

3. *Trim edges straight with sharp knife.*

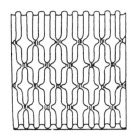

4. *Pinch ribs together in pairs to form the required pattern.*

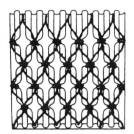

5. *Pipe fine lines over prepared foundation to make honeycomb stitch. This should be done after the panels have been attached to the cake.*

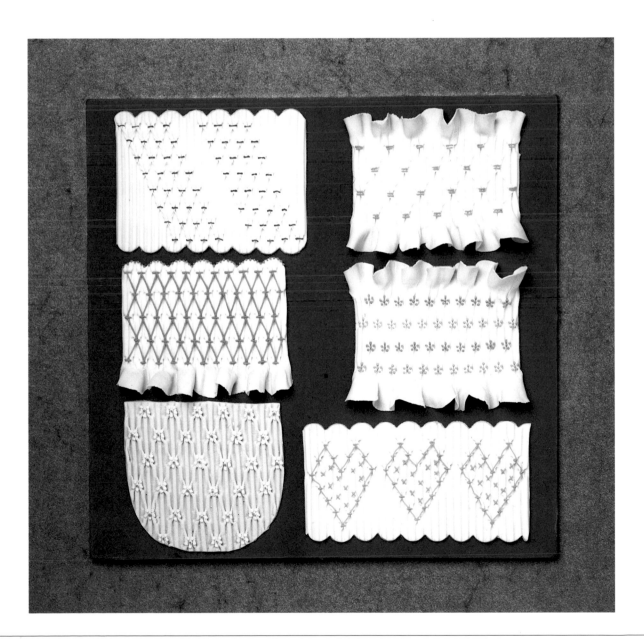

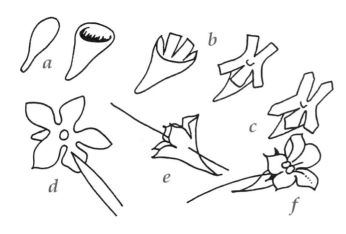

Steps – Ivy Leaved Toadflax

a. Hollowed cone.
b. Petals.
c. Petal edges.
d. Thinning petal.
e. Wire emerging above the spur.
f. Finished flower.

Close-up of smocking panel and floral arrangement.

Ivy Leaved Toadflax

❧ Make a cone shape from a tiny ball of white paste, about ¼" (6mm). Hollow out using a cocktail stick.

❧ Make three cuts at the edge of the hollow tube to form two small petals. Cut a bit deeper either side of the petals and trim a thin wedge from each side to give a greater division between the top petals and the bottom. Now cut the remainder of the cylinder into three sections. Round off the square edges by trimming with small pointed scissors.

❧ Lay the flower on its side and thin the petals by rolling them back and forth with a cocktail stick.

❧ Push a hooked 30g wire through the throat of the flower and exit at the top just above the little pointed tail. Curve back the petals. Pinch the sides of the flower between thumb and finger to bring the petals close together. If the flower is to be dusted with violet petal dust, it should be done at this stage as soon as the flower is dry.

❧ Finally, the honey-guide is made by rolling two very tiny balls of yellow paste. Brush the throat of the flower with egg white and attach the yellow balls close together.

❧ Cut a tiny calyx and mould it around the base of the stem wire.

❧ Make leaves using the smallest size Ivy leaf. Arrange trails of flowers and leaves as in photograph.

Ivy Leaved Toadflax.

Alstroemeria Cake

EQUIPMENT

14" x11" (355 x 280mm) Oval board

Icing tubes (tips) 0 & 1

Paper template for side

½" (12mm) Ribbon board edging

Scriber

MATERIALS

12" x 9" (305 x 230mm) Oval fruit cake

2 ½ lbs (1.25kg) marzipan

Apricot jam, boiled or sieved

3 ½ lbs (1.75kg) Sugarpaste (rolled fondant)

Clear alcohol (Gin or Vodka)

Colours – Christmas red, egg yellow, moss green, darkbrown,black

Royal Icing

Flowers – 3 yellow & brown Alstroemeria, 2 red & yellow Alstroemeria, 3 sprays yellow Freesias, 3 stems of dark green leaves, 4 sprays Lily of the Valley

❧ Shape the cake by cutting away a section with a sharp knife, using (see Template *a*, page 62).

❧ Brush all over with boiled, sieved apricot jam. Cover with marzipan and leave overnight to dry off.

❧ Cover the board with dark brown sugarpaste – use dark brown paste colour, adding a little black. Leave a day or so to dry. To remove the paste from the centre of the board, cut a template to fit the shape of the cake. Place in the centre of the board and cut round it.

❧ Cover the cake with coral red paste – a strong mix of Christmas red with some egg yellow and a very little moss green. Mix the colours thoroughly into a small piece of paste at first, adding varying amounts of the above colours until you achieve the required shade. Add to the main quantity of paste, kneading well to avoid streaking. The colour will be much paler when added to the white paste so be prepared to strengthen it using the same method as before.

❧ Place the cake in position on the board. Cut a paper template (Template *b*, page 62) to fit the sides of the cake. Trace the design onto the template, repeating the pattern by aligning the corner marks. Attach the template to the cake, joining it with masking tape. Scribe over all the lines of the design.

❧ Pipe neat beading around the base of the cake with a N°1 tube (tip).

❧ Pipe over the embroidery lines using dark brown royal icing and a N°. 0 tube (tip).

❧ Stick the ribbon around the edge of the cakeboard.

❧ Arrange the flowers and leaves as in the picture.

❧ Start by binding together two stems of leaves with two sprays of Lily of the Valley and one spray of Freesias. Add one Alstroemeria with bud.

❧ Stick a small piece of brown modelling paste on the board, in the curve of the cake. Take the spray, positioning it at the back nearest to the cake and push the stems into the soft paste. Support this until it stays in place. Make a smaller spray with one stem of leaves and one spray of Freesias. Stick this into the paste and let it trail across the board. Arrange flowers in the centre to make a pleasing shape.

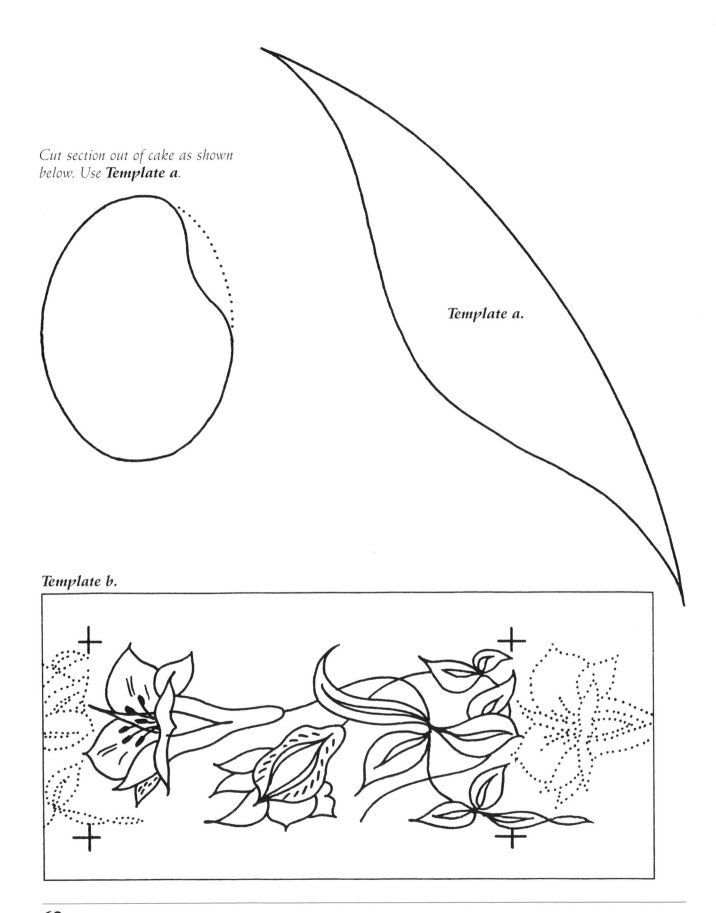

*Cut section out of cake as shown below. Use **Template a**.*

Template a.

Template b.

Alstroemeria

These flowers show many variations in colour. Those with a strong colour such as yellow, red, & orange should be made from paste which is a paler version of that particular colour. The deeper tones are brushed in with dusting powder when the petal is dry. The pale pinks are better to be made in white and lightly dusted with pink. Where the flower is two-coloured, make the petals with the paler colour so that the darker colour can be applied later.

Pistil

❧ Tape a piece of 28g wire with white tape. Cut off the tape leaving about ¼" (6mm) spare. Cut this tape into three sections, twist each one to form a thick thread and curl the ends around a cocktail stick. Tape six stamens around the pistil. Paint the tips a greenish-grey colour.

Petals

❧ Roll out paste with a ridged leaf roller and cut three narrow petals and three wide ones, positioning the cutter so that the ridge is running centrally from the base of the petal to the tip.

Narrow Petals

❧ Thin the petal edges by stroking with a ball tool. Press on a veiner or mark a deep central vein with a veining tool. Cup the areas either side of the vein by turning the petal over and working with a ball tool. Pinch the tip of the petal to emphasise and pull the tip back slightly. Dip a 28g wire into egg white or gum glue and insert into the base of the petal. Repeat with two remaining narrow petals.

Wide Petals

❧ Treat as for the narrow petals but if not using a special veiner, mark a central vein on the front of the petal and on the underside of the petals mark a line either side of the central vein, following the shape of the petal. Wire the petal and leave to dry. Support the sides of the petals so that they do not dry flat and curve the tip back.

❧ Brush the bottom half of two of the narrow petals with yellow. Paint the three narrow petals with maroon flecks. Dust the tips of all petals and shade down the backs with pale green.

❧ Tape two of the narrow petals to the stamens with the two petals overlapping. The stamens should curve away from these petals. Tape the third narrow petal opposite.

❧ Arrange two of the wide petals opposite each other in the gaps, and the third petal behind the narrow overlapping petals. Tape the stem firmly.

Ovary

❧ Take a small ball of paste ¼" (6mm) and slide it over the wire to the base of the flower. Stick to the flower with gum glue. Pinch three ridges in the ovary in line with the centre of the outer petals. Smooth the join with a modelling tool until it blends with the flower.

CUTTERS: Alstroemeria
VEINERS: Alstroemeria

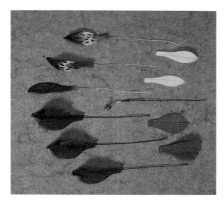

Petal shapes. Stamens wired.   *Petals shaped, veined and wired.*   *Flower coloured and assembled.*

Alstroemeria, close-up.

Lily of the Valley   *Freesia*

a. Take a 4mm ball of white paste. Moisten the tip of a medium stamen (preferably with green stem) with egg white. Insert tip into ball of paste.

a. Roll out white paste very thinly; cut out shapes with a small Lily of the Valley cutter.

a. Paint the tip of the ball with egg white and attach the blossom shape. Push a small pointed tool into the centre of the blossom, this will make a hollow and coax the petals into a cupped shape. Curve the stem so that the flowers will hang attractively.

Buds

a. Roll tiny balls of paste and stick to the tips of the stamens. Curve the stamen cottons by stroking with a finger nail.

a. Cut a piece of 26g wire and tape the flowers to it. Starting with 3 buds, tape them to the main stem leaving short stems. Add five flowers leaving a stem of about ½" (6mm). More buds and flowers may be included if desired.

Lily of the Valley.

Freesia, steps.

Freesias come in many lovely colours; red, pink, yellow, purple, white and the stamens are the same colour as the flower. e.g. If the Freesia is to be white, then white stamens should be used.

Stamens

a. Tape 6 fine stamens, plus one longer stamen for the pistil, to a 28g wire.

The Flower

a. Roll a ball of paste ⅓" (8mm) into a cone *(see* **Hollowing Method**, *page 8)*.

a. Hollow out the cone by inserting a cocktail stick (rounded toothpick) into the bulbous end and rotating it to open up the cone into a cylinder, thinning the walls.

a. To form the petals, cut the edge of the cylinder into six sections with small pointed scissors. Cut off the square corners from the petals. Roll the cocktail stick across each petal to thin and shape.

a. Insert wired stamens into the centre of the flower.

a. Thin the back of the flower by rolling between thumb and finger.

a. For a fully open flower arrange alternate petals towards the centre with the remaining three petals curving downwards.

a. For a half open flower, cup all the petals towards the centre.

a. To make a quick calyx; make two small snips opposite each other at the base of each flower and bud which will represent a calyx with two sepals. When dry, colour this green.

Buds

a. Roll a small ball of paste into a long cone, tapering into a narrow tail. Make the smallest buds green and a few larger ones in the colour of the flower.

a. Tape together buds and flowers starting with the smallest buds and last the wide open flowers.

Summer Wedding

EQUIPMENT

15", 11", 9" (380, 280, 230mm) cake boards

Paintbrush N° 2

Icing tips Nos. 0 & 1

Scriber

Paper for templates

Wax paper or non-stick film

Two flower sprays consisting of 2 large Lilies, 3 small Lilies,1 half open Lily, 5 Cream Roses,10 Stephanotis with buds, 6 sprays Lily of the Valley

Two Ivy trails

Four Freesias

Small leaves

MATERIALS

11", 9", 7" (280,230 180mm) Rich fruit cakes

7 lbs (3.5kg) Sugarpaste (rolled Fondant)

5 ½ lbs (2.75kg) Marzipan

Royal Icing

Apricot jam (boiled or sieved)

Alcohol (Gin or Vodka)

Piping gel

This richly decorated wedding cake is reminiscent of the Victorian fashion of pin-tucked gowns with rather heavy lace decoration and embroidery.

- Brush the cakes with boiled, sieved apricot jam. Cover with marzipan. Leave until firm and dry.

- Cover the cakeboards with sugarpaste. Cut out a circle of paste from the centre of the boards the same size as the cakes.

- Cover the cakes with sugarpaste. Place them in the centre of the boards, securing with a little apricot jam.

- Cut a long narrow template to fit the sides of the cake. Fold into six sections and trace the pattern *(Dia. a)* on to all sections of the template. Place the template around the cake and prick through all main lines onto the cake. Repeat this step on all cakes, making a new template to fit each cake.

Lace

- This lace is meant to be heavy. The leaves at the top of the motif *(Dia.b)* are filled in by piping a dot of icing at the tip of the leaf and gently brushing with a slightly damp brush. The lace pieces are piped with a 0 tube (tip), using Royal icing which does not contain glycerine *(see Lace & Filigree, page 70)*.

Embroidered Border

- Trace the pattern of the floral border *(Dia. c)*. To enable the curved pattern to lie flat over the curved edge of the cake it should be cut in half, the two halves can then be pinned either side of the scallops. Prick or draw an impression of the main points of the design with a scriber. If you scribe too much detail at this stage the pattern may be difficult to follow.

- Mix about ½ teaspoon of piping gel into 4 tablespoons of Royal icing. Work the embroidery with a N° 0 tube (tip) and N° 2 paintbrush *(see Brush Embroidery, page 27)*.

- Tilt the cake away from you and pipe the vertical linework on the side of the cake below the scalloped line. Each group of three lines should have the centre line piped with a N° 1 tube (tip) and overpiped with a N° 0. A N° 0 line is piped either side. Pipe small flowers at regular intervals in the space between the lines.

- Pipe a neat border around the base with a N° 1 tube. Attach lace pieces with small dots of icing above the linework.

- Arrange flowers and lay them on top of the cakes.

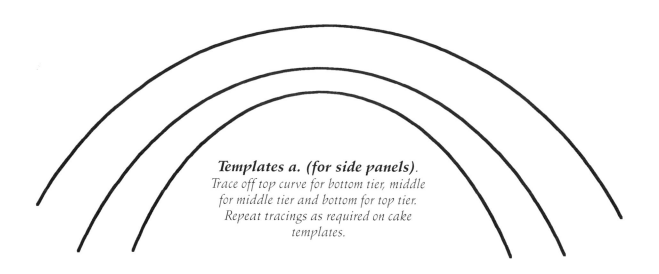

Templates a. (for side panels).
Trace off top curve for bottom tier, middle for middle tier and bottom for top tier. Repeat tracings as required on cake templates.

**Templates c.
(for embroidered borders).**
Trace off top design for bottom tier, middle for middle tier and bottom for top tier. Repeat tracings as required on cake templates.

Above: Lace (Dia. b)

Right: Close up of side panel, Rose and lace design.

Stephanotis Steps.

Stephanotis

❧ Make a Mexican hat shape from a pea-sized ball of white gumpaste *(see **page 8**)*. Thin by rolling with a small knitting needle or a paintbrush handle. Cut out the flower. (This flower has quite sturdy waxy looking flowers so the paste should not be rolled too thin – *see 'steps' on left).*

❧ Press a pointed tool into the centre of the flower. Thin the edges of the petals. Indent the front of the petals.

❧ Push a hooked 28g wire through the flower. Roll the back to form a narrow waist under the petals; the base should be fuller.

❧ Cut a small calyx with a star calyx cutter and pale green paste, thin the tips with a small ball tool. Slip over the base of the flower and stick with egg white or gum glue. Brush the back of the flower pale green.

Quick Rose

❧ Make a cone by rolling a ball of paste until it is pointed at the tip and rounded at the base. Insert a hooked 24g wire into the base. The size of the central cone will depend on the size of the blossom cutter to be used for the petals. To gauge the size, make a cone and lay it in the centre of a cutter with the base in the middle. The tip should be about ¼" (6mm) away from the tip of a petal. It is helpful to allow the cone to dry before adding the petals. To make a bud use one layer only; then add the calyx.

❧ A small rose can be made with two layers. A full rose will require three layers.

❧ Cut out three blossom shapes. Cut down about ¼" (6mm) towards the centre in between petals if using a metal cutter to allow the petals more movement. Keep two of the blossoms under plastic to prevent them drying while working on the first one.

First Layer

❧ Cup each petal by working the centre with a ball tool; soften the edges of the petals with the same tool to thin and give some movement but do not frill. Moisten the Rose centre and one of the petals. Push the wired cone through the middle of the five petals and wrap the first petal around the centre, hiding it completely. Ignore the next petal and moisten the sides of the third petal. Leave the next petal and moisten the fifth petal.

❧ Wrap the third petal around the bud opposite the first. Take the fifth petal, pull up against the bud, forming a spiral and making sure that the petal is not lower than the first one.

❧ Moisten second and fourth petals. Pull each one up around the bud making sure that the centre of each petal covers the join of the third and fifth petals. Ease them to spiral around the bud.

❧ Do not curl back the tips at this stage but open out a little to give more 'air space'.

Second Layer

❧ Take the second blossom shape, cut between the petals and soften and cup as for the first layer. Moisten the centre of the blossom shape. Push the wired first layer through the middle of the blossom shape. Moisten the side of two alternate petals, draw each petal up

Steps – Quick Rose: 1. Central cone; 2. Cut out petals; 3. First layer of petals arranged around centre; 4. Second row of petals in place; 5. Finished Rose.

around the first layer, spiralling them around each other, (the petals in this layer should be slightly higher than the first layer). Moisten one of the three remaining petals, drawing up so the centre of the petal is covering a join. Moisten the side of the petal opposite and overlap the previous petal. Draw up the fifth petal and attach to form a spiral. Slightly curl back the tips and one side of each petal.

Third Layer

❧ Thin the edges of the petals then turn the blossom shape over and cup the petals, this will encourage them to curl back. Attach the petals in random order but set the centre of each petal over a join. Curl back the tips and one side of each petal to look as natural as possible.

Calyx

❧ Make a Mexican Hat shape *(see page 8)* with a medium-sized ball of paste. Thin out by rolling with a short knitting needle or special tool. Cut out calyx with a rose calyx cutter. Make a few snips in the sepals and thin the edges. Hollow the centre. Brush the centre of the calyx with glue and push into position at the base of the flower.

❧ Below the sepals, make a groove all around to shape the ovary. Neaten the base.

Longiflorum Lily

Stamens

🌿 Six stamens are required which have a 'T' shaped tip called the anther. It is now possible to buy these, but if not, alter a regular medium sized stamen by rolling a tiny ball of yellow paste into a cigar shape, moistening the tip of the stamen with egg white and inserting into the centre of the paste, forming a 'T' shape.

Pistil

🌿 Cut a piece of 24g wire and roll a small piece of pale green paste around the tip, allow it to travel down the wire until it covers 1½" (38mm).

Leave a bulbous tip approximately 3mm long. Flatten the top of the pistil and pinch the paste in three sections to form a tricorn shape.

Ovary

🌿 Attach a very small ball of green paste to the base of the pistil; mould around neatly. Using a veining tool, make six evenly spaced indentations in the soft paste.

Assembly

🌿 Set a stamen in each of the six grooves with the heads a little lower than the tip of the pistil. Tape them to the pistil just below the ovary.

Petals

🌿 Cut six pieces of 26 or 28g white wire.

🌿 Roll out white paste thinly using a grooved roller or board.

🌿 Cut three petals from Template **a** and three from Template **b**. While working on the first petal, keep the others under cover (the wider petals **a** are the inside layer, the narrow ones **b** are the outside petals) . Thin the petal **a** edges with a ball tool.

🌿 Vein the petal down the centre, or press on a Lily veiner. Pinch from tip to base to reinforce the crease. Turn the petal over and mark veins on either side of the main vein. Dip wire in egg white and carefully insert into the thickened base of the petal. Curve the tip back. Mould the base of the petal around the stamens and pistil to ensure a good fit when assembling.

🌿 Allow petal to dry with the main part straight and the tip curved back; slightly for a half open flower; more for a full flower. Repeat with the other two petals **a**.

🌿 When dry, dust the base of the inside of the petal with very pale yellow or lime green. Arrange petals evenly around the stamens and tape securely.

🌿 Process petals **b** as before. Before leaving to dry, mould the base of the petals around the half-assembled flower to obtain a good shape. Allow to dry in a natural shape.

🌿 Tape the petals around the first row in between the inner petals.

🌿 Mould a very small ball of pale green paste around the base of the petals, covering the ends of the wires. Smooth down until it is not bulky.

🌿 Tape the wires with green florist's tape. Dust the back of the flower with very pale green.

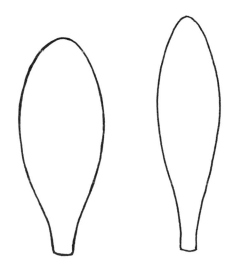

Longiflorum Cutters. a. b.

CUTTERS
Longiflorum Lily.
VEINERS
Lily.

Lily & Rose Shower

Requirements

2 Large Lilies

3 Small Lilies

1 Half-open Lily, 2 buds, 2 leaves

5 Roses

3 Sprays Lily of the Valley

10 Stephanotis with leaves & buds

5 Freesias

3 Trails of small Ivy leaves

❧ This shower bouquet should be loosely arranged using long flower stems, plenty of air space should be left between each flower.

❧ Tape together 1 Lily bud and leaf.

❧ Add in the following order 1 half-open Lily and one spray of Lily of Valley to the left with a leaf opposite; 1 small Lily to left; 1 spray of Stephanotis to the right.

❧ Add 2 Freesias and 1 trail of Ivy to left; 1 small Lily to the centre with 1 Rose and spray of Stephanotis to the left; 2 Freesias at the centre with 1 Rose and bud to the right.

❧ Add a trail of Ivy to right; place 1 large Lily to the left with 1 Rose and Stephanotis to the centre; 1 spray Stephanotis to the right. Add 1 large Lily to the right; tape 3 sprays of Lily of the Valley to the left of the large Lily; add 1 trail of Ivy.

❧ Bend the Lily of Valley and Ivy back to form a return end.

Lily, steps

Top row, left to right:

1. Pistil with stamens.

2. Three inner petals.

3. Three outer petals.

Lower row, left to right:

1. Wired petals.

2. Pistil with inner petals.

3. Finished flower.

*Lily and Rose
Shower (1).*

*Lily and Rose
Shower (2).*

Lily and Rose Shower (3):
completed arrangement.

Heavenly Gardenias

EQUIPMENT

16", 10", 8" (405, 255, 200mm) boards & 1 thin 10" board

Non – stick film

Icing tubes (tips) Nos 1 & 0

Parchment icing bags

Separators-height 6" (152mm) *or* Pillars

Scriber

Paper templates

MATERIALS

14", 10", 8", 6", (355, 255, 200, 150mm) rich fruit cakes or Madeira type

Apricot jam, boiled & sieved

8lbs (4kg) marzipan

Clear alcohol (Gin or Vodka)

10lbs (5kg) Sugarpaste (Rolled fondant)

Filigree ornament *(see p.93)*

Royal Icing

Icing sugar for rolling out

24 Gardenias, sprays of Orange Blossom as required, large glossy leaves

66 Filigree 'Wings'

This ornate cake was inspired by the American style. A 10" cake on a thin 10" board has been placed immediately on top of the 14" base cake. This can easily be removed for cutting by sliding a knife underneath the board. The Gardenias surrounding the second tier, are mounted on wooden cocktail sticks (toothpicks) and were inserted into a thick 'sausage' of sugarpaste which surrounds the base of the cake. Alternatively the cocktail sticks (toothpicks) can be removed before each flower is dry and the flowers attached to the cake with icing.

❧ Brush the cakes with boiled, sieved apricot jam. Cover with marzipan. Leave to dry for a few days. Cover the 16",10" and 8" boards with sugarpaste (rolled fondant). Cut out a circle from the centre of each board, the size of the cake. Brush each cake with alcohol and cover with sugarpaste (rolled fondant). Place the 10" cake on a thin 10" board. Place the other cakes centrally on their boards. Allow the icing time to dry and become firmer, then place the 10"cake on its board on top of the 14" cake, securing with a little Royal icing.

Filigree pieces *(Dia. a)*.

❧ Make 32 for the bottom tier, 18 for the 8" cake and 16 for the 6" cake. The pattern should be placed on a firm board under a piece of non-stick film or wax paper. Pipe the lace first with a '0' tube (tip). Pipe the line surrounding this lace. Pipe the outer line. To flood the outer border, let down a little Royal icing with a few drops of water. Fill in the border with soft icing using a parchment icing bag with a small hole cut in the tip to the size of a Nº 2 tube. Prick any bubbles which might appear. Dry thoroughly in a warm place. To achieve a good sheen, dry under a lamp.

❧ Cut paper templates to fit the sides of each tier. Fold the 14"cake template into 32 sections, 8" into 18, 6" into 16. From the top of each fold, draw a diagonal line *(as Dia. b)*. Place a template around each cake and scribe the fine guideline onto the cake.

❧ Pipe embroidery *(Dia. c)* between each line with Nº 0 tube (tip).

❧ Roll a long 'sausage' of paste about 1" (25mm) thick and long enough to surround the base of the 10" cake, this will form a cushion for flower stems. Stick the cushion in place with a little alcohol.

❧ Arrange flowers and leaves around the top edge of the large cake and either stick in place with royal icing, or, if stems are used, cut off short and insert into the paste cushion.

The flowers will partially cover the side of the 10" cake so no filigree wings are used.

ALL FLOWER STEMS SHOULD BE COMPLETELY CONTAINED IN THIS PASTE AND REMOVED FROM THE CAKE BEFORE CUTTING.

Pipe neat beading around the base of the cakes. Gently remove the filigree 'wings' from the plastic film. Pipe a line of icing along the diagonal lines on the side of the cake. Place each 'wing' on the line positioning approximately 45° to the side of the cake. Repeat all round the cakes (*see Dia. d*).

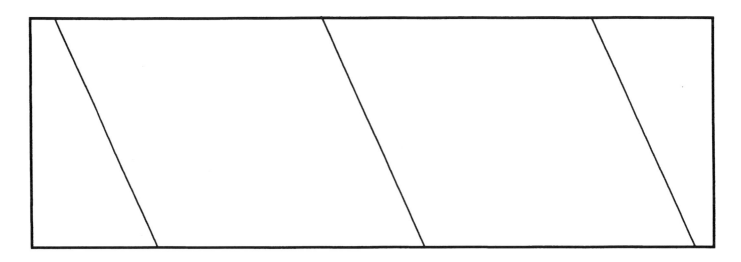

Cake template (Dia. b). *Intervals between the angled lines will vary according to the size of the cake.*

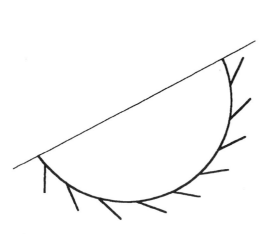

(Dia. d). *Part plan of cake top showing how the 'wings' are set at an angle to the side of the cake.*

Embroidery design (Dia. c).

Filigree design (Dia. a).

Close-up of side of cake showing 'wings', embroidery pattern and flowers in detail.

Gardenia

Although the Gardenia can be made very effectively without wiring, the method given below is for the wired version. This flower will look more interesting when simply arranged with its natural, glossy, dark green leaves; the blossoms should be raised slightly above the leaves.

Small Flower

❧ Make a cone of white gum paste about 15mm or just over half an inch in diameter. Insert a wooden cocktail stick (toothpick) or several thicknesses of wire taped together to support this heavy flower. Cut ridges in the top of the cone to represent closed petals. Pinch each ridge until thin to form the edge of a petal.

❧ Using a medium rose petal cutter, cut out three petals. Tool around the edges to thin and cup the centre. Attach these to the bud, overlapping.

❧ Roll out paste and cut out two medium six-petalled blossom shapes. Cut one shape thicker than the other. Keep the thicker one under a plastic cover to prevent drying out while working on the first shape. Cut petals to shape with a sharp knife.

❧ Thin the edges of the petals by stroking with a ball tool, using more pressure to the right side, making an irregular petal. Curl each petal with a cocktail stick (toothpick).

❧ Push the bud through the centre of the blossom shape. Brush alternate petals with egg white or gum glue and attach to the bud. Repeat with the other three petals, leaving the curled edges free.

❧ Cut the petals of the second blossom as before. Take the second shape and roll each petal lightly to thin and lengthen, then shape and curl petals as before. Brush the centre with glue and cup around the first row of petals. Cut a piece of aluminium foil; push the flower stem through the centre and leave to dry standing in a small wine glass, supported by the foil. Lift the petals slightly and support with small pieces of foam. When dry, lightly dust between petals with pale yellow or lime green.

Large Flower *(Follow instructions for small flower, then proceed as follows):*

❧ Cut two shapes with a large blossom cutter, one thicker than the other. Lightly roll the thicker petals to thin and lengthen them, trim, shape and curl the petals as before. Lay them on a strong piece of foil. Trim and shape the thinner blossom as before. Brush the centre of the first layer of petals with glue and lay the second set on top with each of the petals over a join in the first row. Push the small wired flower through the centre of these petals.

❧ Lift the petals and hold in place with small pieces of foam. Leave the flower to dry with the stem in a small wine glass, supported by the foil. Turn down the edges of the foil if you want the under petals to curl back.

Calyx

Cut out a shape with a small six-petal blossom cutter; cut the petals into points. Slide over the stem and attach with a gap of approximately ½" (15mm) from the back of the flower. Usually it is not necessary to make a calyx because the flower is so large that the calyx does not show at all (alternatively, the calyx could be made using the Hollowing Method *(see **page 8**)*.

Gardenia, steps.

Top row, left to right:

1. Petals.   2. Petals, trimmed.
3. Petals, trimmed and shaped.

Centre: Three inside petals.

Bottom row:

1. Centre.   2. Petals, shaped.
3. Finished flower.   4. calyx.   5. Bud.

Orange Blossom

This fragrant white flower has prominent brown tipped stamens, joined at the base but dividing at the tip.

Centre

Roll a 3 mm ball of pale green flower paste into a tiny club-shape with a bulb at the tip. Insert a 28g wire.

Stamens

Cut out a strip of thinly rolled white paste about ¾" (18mm) long by ½" (15mm) wide. Shred one long edge finely (like a comb). Moisten the long uncut edge with egg white and wrap around the pistil. Brush the tips of the stamens with egg white and dip in ground maize (cornmeal) coloured brown.

Cut out the petals with a Stephanotis cutter or a small five-sepalled calyx cutter. Thin the edges of the petals, vein and cup them.

Insert the centre and mould the petals around the stamens. Cut a calyx with a very small star calyx cutter. Shape and attach to the back of the flower.

CUTTER
Stephanotis

Orange Blossom, steps

***Top row, left to right: 1.** Centre. **2.** Stamens wrapped around centre. **3.** Shaped petals. **4.** Completed flower.*

***Bottom row, left to right: 1.** Paste stamens. **2.** Petals.*

Lacy Wedding Cake

Filigree panels transform these square cakes into unusual shapes with little alcoves for the flowers on the sides.

☙ Brush the cakes with boiled, sieved apricot jam. Cover with marzipan. Leave until marzipan surface is firm and dry. Apply two coats of Royal icing to the cakes. Spread icing smoothly over the boards.

Bottom Tier

☙ Trace **Template a** and place on a firm board under non-stick film. You will require 4 panels as in **Template a** and 4 in reverse. Pipe over the pattern using a N⁰· 1 tube (tip) for veins and stems and a N⁰· 2 for outlining flower and leaves. Pipe the border lines with a N⁰· 1 tube. Let down a little icing with water until it is the consistency of unwhipped cream. Cut a small hole in the tip of a small parchment icing bag the size of a N⁰· 2 tube, fill in the spaces between flowers and leaves with a thin layer of icing, using a fine brush to coax the icing into small corners. Flood the border, building it up to make a cushioned effect. Make three more sections the same.

☙ Turn the pattern over and draw in the outlines of the reverse image on the back. Make four sections with this pattern.

Top Tier

☙ Repeat above using **Template b.**

Collar

☙ Place the pattern on a board under non-stick film. Outline all edges with a N⁰· 1 tube (tip). Flood the collar with softened icing. Dry thoroughly. Pipe rose motif in the corners. Pipe dots around the edge with a N⁰· 1 tube (tip) to form a picot edge before removing from the film. Leave until dry.

Curved Middle Sections

☙ Cut out thinly rolled pastillage (see recipe, page **6**) with **Template c**. Dry over a curved object until it is firm but still flexible. (e.g. Drinks can or small rolling pin).

☙ Using board **Template d** and a scriber, mark guidelines for the panels. Pipe a line with a N⁰· 1 tube (tip) around the curve which you will have marked on the board at the centre of one side of the cake. Position the curved pastillage section on the line, bending it slightly if necessary to fit the line on the board. Support it and repeat on the other three sides.

Lace Panels

☙ The rose motif should be nearest to the centre in all cases. Use the reverse panel for the opposite side of the curved section. Pipe a line on the board from the edge of the curved panel to the corner of the cake. Attach the first lace panel by piping a line of icing down the side edge and attaching this to the side of the pastillage curve. Support with a small block until set. Pipe another line on the board running from this lace panel to the next pastillage curve.
Pipe a line down both sides of the next lace panel and position it on the board with one edge butted against the previous piece and the other edge to the pastillage curve.

☙ Carefully remove the collar from the backing. Pipe a line around the top edge of the of the lace panels. Lift the collar and position it centrally on the cake, supported by the panels.
Pipe curtain work between the top of the cake and the inner edge of the collar. Neaten all joins between the lace panels with small dots piped with a N⁰· 1 tube (tip). Repeat these instructions for the 2nd cake.

☙ Arrange small posies of flowers in the alcoves and decorate the top tier with an ornament or flowers.

Top ornament (*see* **page 95**)

EQUIPMENT

14", 9" (355,230mm) Boards

Icing tubes (tips) 2,1,0

Wax paper or non-stick film

Parchment paper bags

Paintbrush

MATERIALS

10", 6" (255,150mm) square cakes

4lbs (2kg) Marzipan

Boiled sieved apricot jam

2lbs (1 kg) Royal Icing

Small amount Pastillage

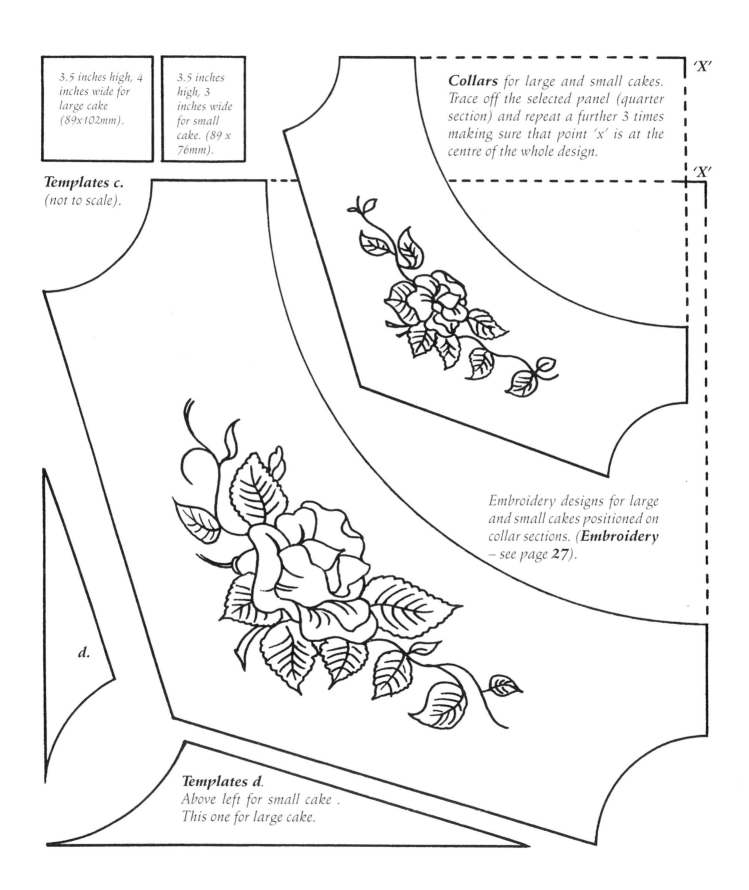

3.5 inches high, 4 inches wide for large cake (89x102mm).

3.5 inches high, 3 inches wide for small cake. (89 x 76mm).

Templates c.
(not to scale).

Collars for large and small cakes. Trace off the selected panel (quarter section) and repeat a further 3 times making sure that point 'x' is at the centre of the whole design.

'X'

'X'

Embroidery designs for large and small cakes positioned on collar sections. (**Embroidery** – see page **27**).

d.

Templates d.
Above left for small cake .
This one for large cake.

Template a – for large cake.

Template b – for small cake.

Close-up of cake showing alcove for floral arrangement.

Leafy Borders

EQUIPMENT

12" (305mm) square board

Icing tubes (tips)
0 & 1

Wax paper or non-stick film

Tracing paper

Scriber

MATERIALS

8" (200mm) square cake

1½ lbs (750g) Marzipan

Boiled sieved apricot jam

2lbs (1kg) Royal Icing*

Blue liquid colour

The Royal icing used for collars should not contain glycerin.

🍃 Brush the cake with boiled, sieved apricot jam. Cover with marzipan. Place on the centre of the board and leave until the surface of the marzipan is dry. Apply two coats of blue Royal icing. When dry, ice the board surrounding the cake.

Collars

🍃 Trace off the pattern for the plain under-collar *(Dia a)*. Place under non-stick film. Using blue icing, outline the collar with a N°. 1 tube (tip). Let down the remaining icing by adding water until the consistency is like unwhipped cream. Half fill a large parchment bag, without a tube (tip). Cut a hole in the end the size of a N°. 2 tube. Evenly fill in the collar with soft icing, pricking any bubbles which may appear. Dry under a lamp to achieve a good sheen.

🍃 Trace the pattern for the leafy top collar *(Dia. b)*. Place on a board and cover with non-stick film.

🍃 Using white icing and a N°. 1 tube, pipe the leaf veins and outline. Pipe around the outside edge of the collar. Carefully fill in the spaces with soft icing, using a fine brush if necessary to coax the icing into narrow corners. Dry thoroughly.

Board Collar

🍃 Cut out the template of a quarter collar section *(Dia. c)*. Place on the board at the corner of the cake. Using a scriber, mark around the edge of the template and outline the leaf shape. Repeat with remaining corners. (The quarter collar sections should meet in the middle of each side, forming one complete collar).

🍃 Pipe outline of the base collar with a N°. 1 tube (tip) in white icing directly on to the board.

🍃 Pipe veins and leaves. Flood spaces with softened icing. Leave to dry. Pipe neat beading around the base of the cake.

🍃 Pipe a picot edge around the base and the under collar with a N°. 1 tube (tip). As shown in diagram.

🍃 Carefully remove the under-collar and the lace collar from the film. Apply a few dots of icing to the underside of the leafy top-collar and lay this in place on the under-collar.

🍃 Pipe a line of icing around the edge of the cake. Lower the collars, adjusting them until they are centrally positioned.

🍃 Place flowers of your choice or pipe a message in the centre.

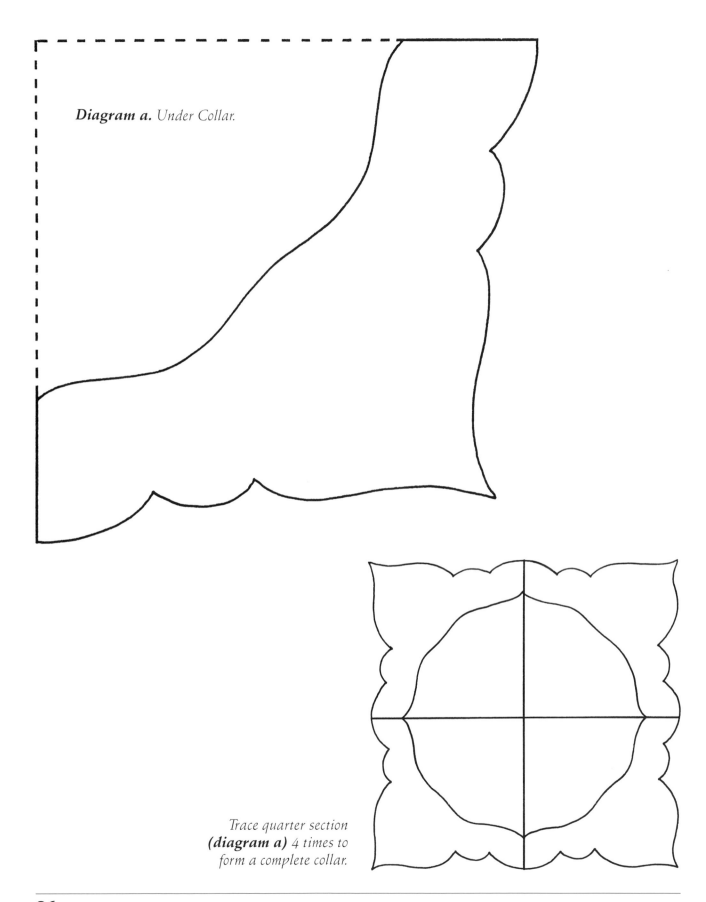

Diagram a. *Under Collar.*

Trace quarter section
(diagram a) *4 times to*
form a complete collar.

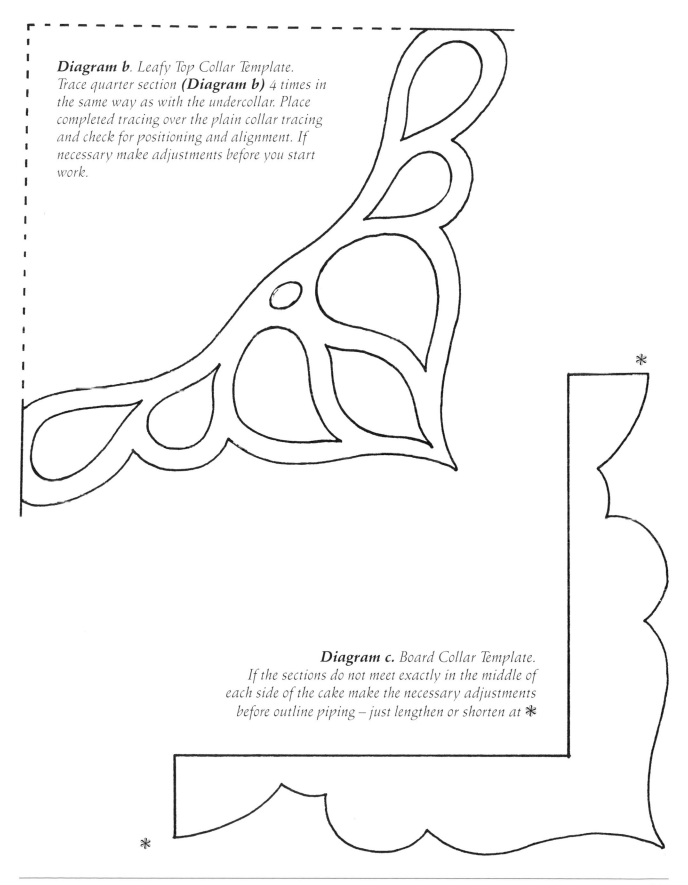

Diagram b. *Leafy Top Collar Template.*
*Trace quarter section **(Diagram b)** 4 times in*
the same way as with the undercollar. Place
completed tracing over the plain collar tracing
and check for positioning and alignment. If
necessary make adjustments before you start
work.

Diagram c. *Board Collar Template.*
If the sections do not meet exactly in the middle of
each side of the cake make the necessary adjustments
before outline piping – just lengthen or shorten at ✳

Contrasts

EQUIPMENT

13" x 11" (330 x 280mm) oval board.

Oval plaque cutter

Paint brushes – 0,1 & 2

Rolling pin

Icing tubes (tips) Nos. 0,1 & 2

Cutters – Medium Blossom, Petunia, Small Circle

1 metre fine black ribbon for cake

1.25 metres Black ribbon for board

Paper template

Scriber

Tile or palette

MATERIALS

10" x 8" (255 x 200mm) oval cake

Apricot jam, boiled and sieved

2½ lbs (1.25kg) Marzipan

Clear alcohol (Gin or Vodka)

3½ lbs (1.75kg) Sugarpaste

Black food colouring

Small amount of Royal Icing

Icing Sugar (Confectioner's) for rolling out

8oz (250g) Pastillage *(see p.6)*

❧ **Silhouettes** – Great care is required when painting silhouettes as the slightest smudge would spoil the effect. An easy method is to paint the design on a plaque before applying to the cake.

❧ **Plaque** – Roll out modelling paste to ¼" (6mm) thick. Cut out shape with plaque cutter. Leave to dry thoroughly. Transfer the picture *(Dia. a)* onto the plaque. Spread a little black food colour onto a tile or palette. Paint the outlines and all fine lines with size 0 brush. Infil with even strokes and a size 2 brush. Use only the minimum amount of water with the colour.

❧ Brush the cake with boiled, sieved apricot jam. Cover with almond paste. Cover the board with sugarpaste and leave for 1–2 days.

❧ Brush the sides but not the top of the cake with alcohol.

❧ Cover cake with sugarpaste, smoothing carefully. Cut out and remove a shape from the sugarpaste on top of the cake, using the same cutter which was used to cut the plaque. Carefully lift the silhouette plaque and place it in position on top of the cake.

❧ Smooth the cake top until it fits neatly around the edge of the plaque.

❧ Cut a paper template to fit around the sides of the cake. Fold into six sections. Draw the linework pattern *(Dia. b)* on one section. Trace this onto the other sections.

❧ Place the template around the cake. Scribe the linework guide onto the cake.

❧ Pipe beading around the base of the cake with a N⁰ 1 or 2 tube (tip).

❧ Tilt cake away from you. Pipe the first line with N⁰ 2 tube (tip). Overpipe the first line with a N⁰ 1 and pipe another N⁰ 1 line just below it. Overpipe these lines with N⁰ 0 and pipe another N⁰ 0 line just below. Mix a small amount of black icing. Pipe dots around plaque with 0 tube (tip).

❧ Cut out flower shapes *(Dia. c)* with a blossom cutter in black and white. Thin the edges and stick the black shapes to the cake, in the centre of each scallop. Tool the white blossom shape to curve and attach to the centre of the black petals. Cut a small black round shape and stick it in the centre of the white blossom. Paint stems and leaves with black food colour.

❧ Transfer board design *(Dia. d)* onto the board and position between the flowers on the side of the cake. Outline the leaves and paint the stems with black colouring as for the cake using a N⁰ 0 brush. Fill in the leaves with a N⁰ 2 brush. Make black and white flowers as before and stick in the centre of the leaves.

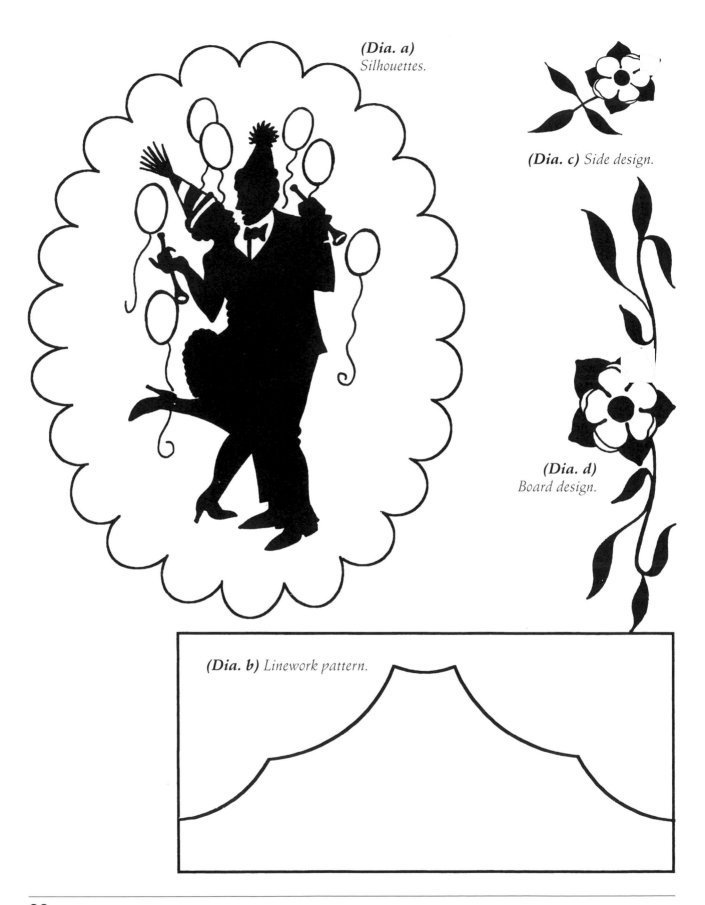

(Dia. a) *Silhouettes.*

(Dia. c) *Side design.*

(Dia. d) *Board design.*

(Dia. b) *Linework pattern.*

Cake Top Ornaments

A sugar ornament for the top tier of a wedding cake will add distinction to a well-designed cake. Being smaller than the top tier, it will add grace, height and elegance to the lines of the cake and the chosen ornament should compliment the overall shape of the cake.

The various shapes of bells, crowns, rings, doves, decorative flower vases are all symbolic of a special occasion.

The bases and some of the foundation pieces of the ornaments featured are made with run-out pieces of Royal icing. These can be successfully made with Pastillage, using the patterns provided.

Bell Ornament

Bases *(see Dias. a & b)*

🙠 Make one large and one small base. Pipe outline with No 0 tube (tip) and medium peak icing. Half fill parchment bag with run-out consistency icing. Cut hole the size of a Nº 2 tube, flood generously within the outline until the icing is cushioned well. Dry both bases in a warm place to achieve a nice glossy finish. When dry stick together with icing sugar and pipe Picot edges with a Nº 0 tube (tip).

Bell Sections

Six required (see Dia. c)

🙠 Place the pattern under wax paper or non-stick film. First, pipe the latticework in the centre with a No 0 tube (tip). Pipe a line around it.

> ### MATERIALS
>
> Icing tube (tip) Nº 0 or 1
>
> Parchment bags
>
> Non-stick film
>
> Flat board
>
> Small amount medium peak Royal icing
>
> Icing of run-out consistency
>
> Small cluster of moulded flowers

🙠 Pipe an outer line. Flood border between the two outer lines. Make a spare piece in case of breakage.

🙠 Leave to dry thoroughly.

🙠 Remove pieces from non-stick film. Turn over. Pipe a line with a Nº 0 tube (tip) around the edge of the lattice and also around the outer edge. Flood as in side one to neaten the underside which will be visible when the ornament is finished. Repeat on all pieces. Dry.

🙠 **Assembly** – Scribe six equally spaced lines around the edge of the base, meeting in the centre. Pipe a little icing on the bottom of the first section and place into position on one of the scribed lines. Support in an upright position with small blocks. Stick second section opposite and join tops together where they meet with neat dots of icing. Repeat adding two more sections either side. The tops of each piece should join together to form a small crown.

🙠 N.B. As the space in the centre of the ornament is small, the flower arrangement must be made up of quite small flowers. It is easier to judge the correct size of the arrangement if it is started after the first half of the bell is assembled. Place a small piece of modelling paste in the centre, feed in small trails of flowers between each filigree piece, sticking the wires into the paste. Put central flowers in place taking care not to break the lattice work. Now stick the remaining upright pieces into place with a little Royal icing. When dry, add trails of flowers between these pieces, sticking them into the paste.

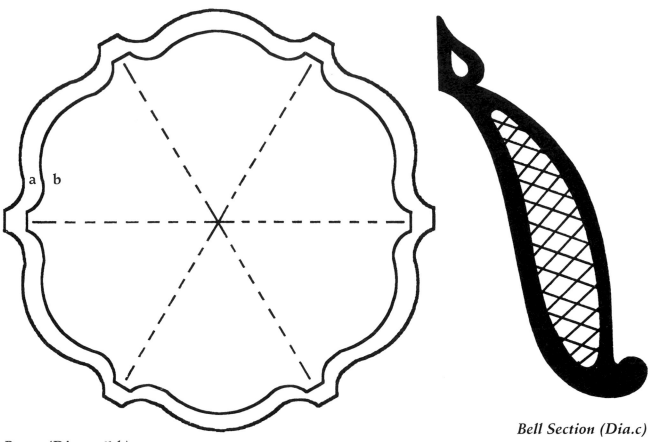

Bases (Dia. a & b)
Arrange Bell Sections as shown by the dotted lines.

Bell Section (Dia.c)

Close-up of Bell Ornament.

Filigree Flower Vase

❧ Using **patterns a & b**, make two run-out pieces from each pattern. Outline one shape with a N°· 0 tube (tip). Flood the centre with let-down icing , the consistency of cream; filling generously to give a cushioned effect. Run out the other three sections the same. (It should be noted that two sections are slightly wider than the others.)

❧ The base sections **c & d** should be outlined and flooded in the same manner. When dry stick **base c** onto **base d**.

❧ When all the pieces are dry, mark diagonal lines on sections **a & b** from the top left-hand corner, following the guide line. Embroider the design on the bottom half. Mark a small square centrally on the base, using the pattern as a guide. Pipe a decorative picot edge or connected dots around edge of both bases.

❧ Assemble the vase by piping along the bottom of one of the narrower sections **(b)**. Stick the first section in position along one of the lines marked on the base. Support in an upright position Stick the other narrow section on the line opposite. Pipe

a line down each side and the bottom edge of the wider section **(a)**. Stick this on the base line and against the edges of **(b)**. Repeat with second section **(a)**. Adjust until all the sides are neatly joined top and bottom.

❧ You should now have a square structure tapering at the top to a smaller square. Pipe neat beading around the bottom to neaten the join.

Filigree Wings
(4 wings will be required).

❧ Lay a piece of non-stick film over the pattern. Pipe filigree design with a N°· 0 or 1 tube (tip), insuring that all the lines are touching). Pipe outline. Pipe an outer line and flood a border between the two outer lines. Make an extra piece in case of breakage.

❧ When dry, stick all four 'wings' to the marked diagonal lines on the vase. Support until dry.

❧ Pipe a neat edge or add lace to the top edge

Pattern b.

Filigree Wing.

Wings fixed to diagonal line on both a. & b.

Pattern a.

***Filigree Flower Vase**. Large and small bases. Centre square for location of vase.*

d c

Filigree Vase.

Filigree Leaves

🍃 Make one large and one small base, one complete section *(Template a)* two half sections *(Template b)*.

🍃 Lay pattern *a* and *b* under a piece of non-stick film or wax paper. With Royal icing and a Nº 0 tube (tip) pipe the veins of the leaves, then outline them neatly. Pipe the double outer lines. Let down a little icing until it is the texture of unwhipped cream. Place in a small parchment bag with no tube, cut off the tip the size of a Nº 2 tube (tip), carefully flood the outside border. Dry under gentle heat for a shiny finish.

🍃 Repeat with remaining sections. Leave to dry.

❧ Turn the filigree pieces over and outline the border on the underside with a Nº 0 tube (tip). Flood border with softened icing as before. Dry.

❧ Pipe a neat row of dots all around the outer edges leaving the straight edge of the half sections plain.

❧ Outline and flood the bases ***(Templates c & d)***. When dry, stick base ***c*** onto base ***d*** then pipe small dots all round the edges.

Assembly

❧ Pipe a neat line of icing down the straight edge of a half section, Attach to the central line of the complete section. Attach the other half section opposite and support until dry.

❧ Pipe a line of icing on the bottom of each section and place centrally on the ornament base.

❧ Add flowers in between each section.

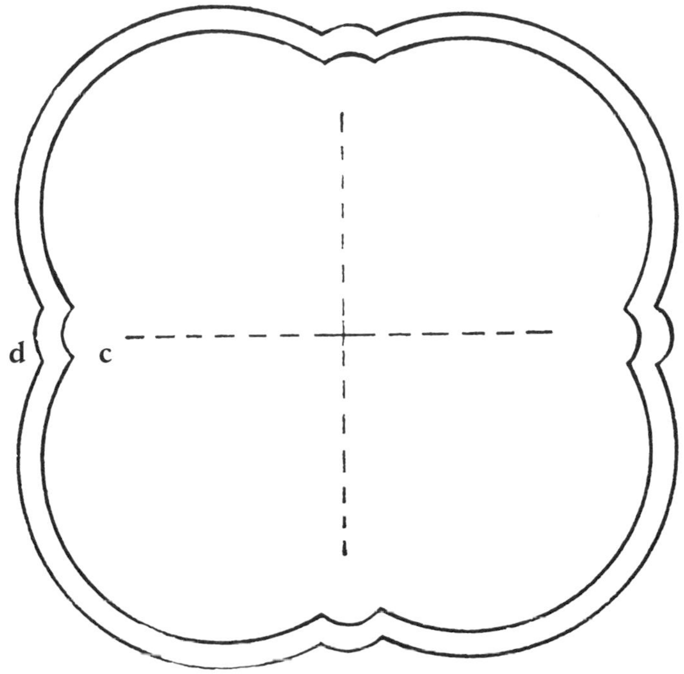

Templates d & c: Filigree Leaves
– bases, large & small.

Filigree Leaves.

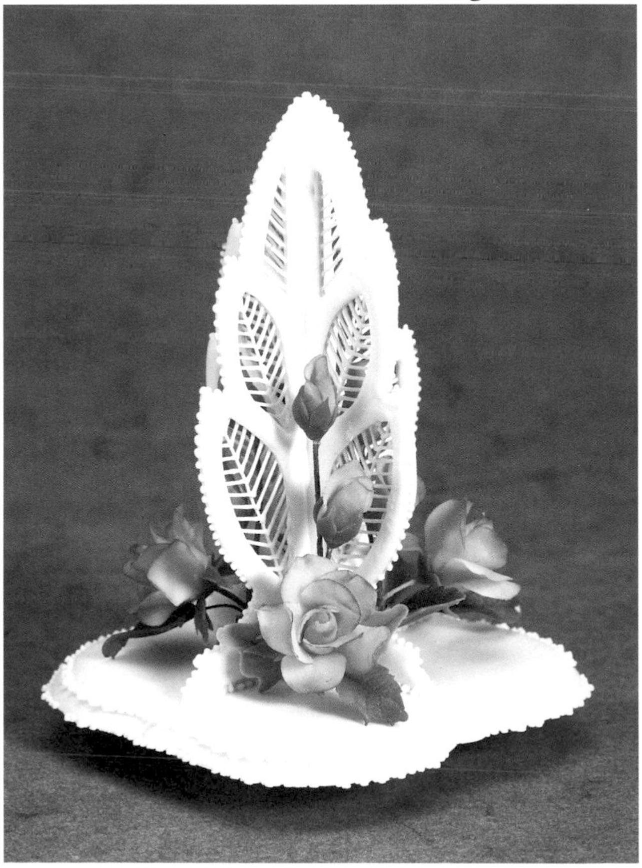

Filigree Leaf Templates

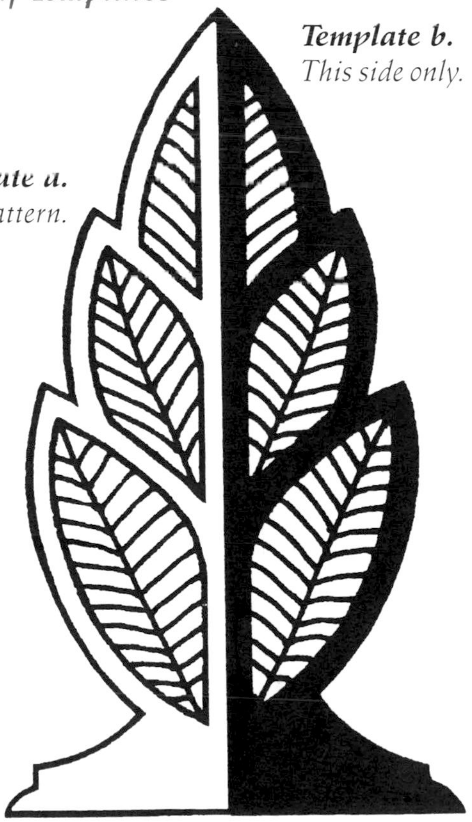

Template b.
This side only.

Template a.
Whole pattern.

ACKNOWLEDGEMENTS

The Author would like to thank the following for their assistance.

Cake Art Ltd., Venture Way, Crown Estate, Priorswood, Taunton, TA2 8DE.

Great Impressions, Greenlea, 14 Studley Drive, Swarland, Morpeth,
Northumberland, NE65 9JT.

Jem Cutters, PO Box 115, Kloof, 3640, Natal, South Africa.

Orchard Products, 51 Hallyburton Road, Hove, East Sussex, BN3 7GP.

J.F. Renshaw Ltd., Crown Street, Liverpool, L8 7RF.

Squires Kitchen, 3 Waverley Lane, Farnham, Surrey, GU9 8BB.

Sugarflair Colours, Brunel Road, Manor Trading Estate,
Benfleet, Essex, SS7 4PS.